LOVE OF THE WORLD
Meditations
by
R.E.C. Browne

LOVE OF
THE WORLD

Meditations by
R. E. C. Browne
Edited by
Ian Corbett
with a Biographical Introduction by
Richard Hanson

CHURCHMAN PUBLISHING
1986

LOVE OF THE WORLD
by
R. E. C. Browne
was first published in 1986 by
Churchman Publishing Limited
117 Broomfield Avenue
Worthing
West Sussex
BN14 7SF
and distributed to the book trade by
Bailey Bros. of Swinfen Limited
Warner House
Folkestone
Kent
CT19 6PH.
ISBN 1 85093 036 8

Made and printed by
Whitstable Litho Limited

CONTENTS

PREFACE

When I moved to be rector of the parish of St. John Chrysostom, Manchester, in July 1975 I soon became aware of the benign shadow of Charlie Browne, a former incumbent from 1953 to 1959, whose funeral service had been conducted in the church only weeks before I arrived. He was spoken of with warmth and affection by parishioners, and I discovered he had been of incalculable help and support to many of my brother clergy. Like so many of my contemporaries, I was amazed by the wisdom, insight and vision of his 'Ministry of the Word', which was reissued by S.C.M. Press in 1976 and again in 1984, having originally been published in 1958.

Charlie's widow, Mary, continued to be very active in the parish, and disclosed to me the full extent of his unpublished notes, letters and papers. A friend of Charlie's, Dr. Michael Wilson, formerly of Birmingham University, first mooted the idea of publishing and collected from others a number of further writings. It was clear that from this wealth of material could be extracted much that was of permanent value, and so a labour of love began for me that continued well beyond my moving from the parish in 1980. There were certainly considerable difficulties: there was much overlapping of material, some of it was in uncertain order, and deciphering that belonging to the period of the onset of Parkinson's disease was problematic. But a body of reasonably complete papers eventually emerged, requiring relatively little editing or alteration.

Their order here owes nothing to the author. They fall into several categories, which are indicated by the section headings. It is not often possible to date them precisely, though most of them belong to the 1950s and were obviously spoken to groups of clergy. Hence, those readers expecting the highly polished and refined manner of the earlier book may at times be disappointed, though both the economy and trenchancy of style remain. Some papers were clearly finished products, others would certainly have been worked on further for publication. It has been felt advisable to leave them with minimal editorial interference rather than risk the task of rewriting. One or two quotations are unattributed: perhaps readers can provide references? The 'Meditations on the Temptations and Passion' were previously published by S.C.M. Press, and I am grateful to them for allowing their inclusion here.

I am immensely indebted to Mary Browne for her help, encouragement, and painstaking examination of the manuscript; and we are deeply grateful to Miss Winifred Marsden, Miss Sheila Ralphs and Miss Raine Cully for assisting her; to Professor Ronald Preston for advice on presentation and editing; to former associates of Charlie Browne, the Revd. Dr. Michael Wilson, the Revd. Anthony Hill, the Revd. Martin Down, the Revd. Canon Bob McDermott, the Revd. Dr. John Turner and the Revd. Canon Frank Wright, for their support and, in several cases, supplying material; and to Mrs. Ruth Fingerhut and her colleagues at the University of Salford for typing it. We hope that you can now share in our enrichment and enlightenment.

Ian D. Corbett
Honorary Canon of Manchester

BIOGRAPHICAL INTRODUCTION

Charles Browne was born in Belfast in 1906, where his father was a Church of Ireland rector. His family came from Co. Sligo, but all his youth and his education up to university level were spent in Belfast. He graduated from Dublin University (Trinity College, Dublin) in 1928 and was ordained in 1929, and spent the next twelve years working as a curate and then curate-in-charge in Church of Ireland parishes in Belfast. In spite of this long residence in the North of Ireland, his speech never betrayed an Ulster accent. But certainly the Church of Ireland can claim to have formed him. That Church usually produces fairly conventional and recognisable types, but every now and then it throws up somebody of unusual and remarkable character and mind. We recall Jonathan Swift, Patrick Brontë, J.N. Darby (founder of the Plymouth Brethren), Robert Dolling, George Tyrrell, William Magee. Irish Anglicans (or Anglican-bred Irishmen) like these are unclassifiable; they fall into no recognised category. Of such was Charles Browne. Nobody could describe him as Evangelical or Anglo-Catholic or Modernist, though he had traits of all these. Perhaps the production of people like this is encouraged in Ireland because it is the scene of the collision of two cultures much more intensely than in England. Such a collision seems to produce originality and sometimes even genius.

For four years (1942-1946) Charles Browne was chaplain of St. Columba's College, an Anglican public school situated in the hills above Dublin, founded under the inspiration of the Oxford Movement in the eighteen-forties. For another three years he was Theological Colleges' Secretary of the Student Christian Movement, based on London. In both these posts the intellectual interests, which were predominant in his character, were given fuller expression. But at St. Columba's he was no wishy-washy highbrow eschewing sport. He took a full part in coaching for Rugby football (which he had continued to play himself for a long time during his years in Belfast) and cricket. Once again, one sees that he answers to no easy classification. In 1948, while still an S.C.M. Secretary, he married, and his wife, Mary, was for the rest of his life his great supporter, confidante and finally nurse. Early in the 1950's, stimulated by his wife's painting and encouragement, though he himself had never painted in his life, he found a new way of expressing his spirituality with an astonishing freedom. This became a great interest and relaxation for the next ten years or so. He would have found it impossible to depict anything visible merely to the physical eye but painted entirely from within, drawing on a rich store of visual memories.

From 1949 to 1953 he was rector of a tough, working-class parish in one of the less pleasantly landscaped parts of outer Manchester, All Saints, West Gorton, and from 1953 to 1959 rector of a parish nearer the city centre, in a district where the personality and capacity of the incumbent alone can attract worshippers, St. Chrysostom, Victoria Park. In 1959 he had to retire owing to Parkinson's disease. And on Ascension Day 1975 he died.

On the face of it, this was a very ordinary career. Certainly destiny did not hand out many sweets to Charles Browne and he benefitted from no reliance on vested interests nor acquaintance with the great or influential. But he was no ordinary man, as those who in Ireland or London or Manchester became acquainted with him soon found out. He had a fine, dry, ironic sense of humour, and a smile which included both the mischievous and the engaging. His whole attitude to life, indeed, might be described as ironic in the sense that Socrates and Kierkegaard used the word. Clear insight and rigorous thinking were his distinguishing marks. Sentimentality, cant and hypocrisy he loathed, and he could detect them sooner than most. Neither a cliché nor a platitude ever passed his lips, except to be mocked at.

Words were his great preoccupation through all his life. This does not mean that he had a great flow of oratory; on the contrary, his speech, including his sermons, tended to be laconic, almost Delphic, leaving the hearer to see the connections and pick up the nuances, if he could. He was interested in words in a much deeper sense than as rhetoric. He was concerned about meaning and the use of words, and of that which lies beyond words but is hinted at by words. He was a great student of poetry, especially of modern poetry. He would probably have agreed with Coleridge that poetry is the best words in the best order and not with Wordsworth's definition of it as emotion recollected in tranquillity. His best-known work, *The Ministry of the Word*, in a manner sums up his life. This is no little volume of helpful hints about preaching but a profound study of the meaning and use of language in relation to theology and to faith, and one which will outlast all the ephemeral booklets about how to preach. Charles Browne was not so much interested in what you preach as in how the words which you use in preaching are related to your own thought, and indeed to your whole life, but above all to truth. He was a student of religious language about ten years before the study of religious language became a fashionable occupation. His writing was not facile or showy. It was original, profound and thought-compelling.

Charles was also, and pre-eminently, a man of faith. He was certainly not a charismatic personality, and would have adequately scarified in his hesitant but deadly utterances the more superficial manifestations of the Charismatic Movement. He did not wear his faith on his sleeve. He was in fact one of the exponents of a peculiarly Anglican type of piety, a type which dislikes show and public utterances about faith, which does not easily talk about itself, but which is no less real and strong and vital than the most extroverted and demonstrative religion. What impressed one most about Charles Browne's religion was its depth. It arose out of rigorous and careful thought, thought which evaded no difficulty and stopped short at no conclusion which seemed to be true. It was refined by suffering and enriched by varied experience. Many who sought his counsel informally or formally, during his ministry and in the days of his retirement, almost to the end of his life, learnt from it.

The chief feature in the faith of Charles Browne was the transcendence and glory of God. His apprenticeship in Belfast, that great emporium for the exploitation of religious experience, had left him with a lasting suspicion of man-centred religion, of all activism and emphasis upon administration and finance which tended to obscure care for the gospel and for the communication of the gospel. In fact he disliked systematisation and neat plans, whether theological or pastoral. His writings show how entirely he accepted the brokenness, the insufficiency, of human endeavour and human intentions. He would have agreed with Berkeley that rational happiness is not to be had in this life. But behind his sometimes cynical and always realistic language lay strong conviction, the stronger for being not easily and not often openly expressed. His belief embraced and overcame doubt. To read the writings which he left behind him is to find a large reservoir of faith from which others can draw, the testament of a wise man of God.

R.P.C. Hanson
(Recently Assistant Bishop in the Diocese of Manchester
and Professor of Theology at Manchester University)

INTRODUCTION

Doing Theology

How do we think theologically; or, how do we do theology? Is theology to be considered as a subject for study or as a discipline of mind? Is doctrine definitive or descriptive? Does Christian doctrine tell us exactly what to think about God and man, or does it show us how to think of God and man? In other words, is "God is our father" a literal statement of fact or a simile? Does a theologian's thought proceed from the known to the unknown, or does it proceed from the partially known to the less partially known? Or to put this in another way, does theological thinking move in a straight line out into unknown territory, or does it circle round and round its subject making such reports as can be made?

What happens to a theologian who restricts himself to theologising about theology instead of thinking theologically about all things, events and people? What would happen to a theologian who does not submit to the discipline of his immediate needs? In our age, profound theologising is likely to begin with the theologian's attempts to keep in touch with himself in a quickly changing world of thought and custom.

Men sometimes perish through neglect of the obvious. A theologian must continually pay attention to the way he is using simple, familiar terms such as 'church' and 'world'. Each Christian lives in both, and is to be on his guard against thinking and talking about them as if they are separate from one another. Both church and world have their origin in God; they live and move and have their being in him. Christians are not to leave the world but love it as God loves it; that is, not in a vague, general, benign way, but by respecting individuals and institutions. For example, a Christian is to respect schools and universities as part of God's ceaseless creative activity. How can a theologian take the doctrine of creation truthfully if he limits his field of attention to one particular sphere of life?

The last paragraph might be brought towards a conclusion by certain reflections. From the philosopher a theologian learns to respect honesty in thinking; from the poet, precision in speech; from the scientist, love of truth; from the dramatist, recognition of the movements in human situations. Psychologists and sociologists help him to understand himself and the many groups to which he belongs. These reflections should include reference to all that physicists have done to enlarge us through their discoveries concerning matter, speed and space. Those who fear these achievements might do well to remember that in the legend of David and Goliath, David's intelligence enabled him to defeat the giant's sheer physical power – or if you like, the story celebrates the victory of science over brute force and ignorance.

What a poet says of the man of letters partly describes the work of a theologian – "He must do first what he has always done: he must re-create for his age the image of man, and he must propagate standards by which other men may test that image, and distinguish the false from the true." Can he even begin this unless he is learning as much as he can from artists, scientists and philosophers? How can he learn if he closes himself up in a little group deep within the church? How can he do this learning if he is wandering in a no-man's land somewhere between the active life of the church and the active life of the world?

Are Christians more concerned with moral goodness than with the truth? Does the self-examination of a theologian sometimes bring to light a fear of intellectuals and artists as well as of serious agnostics? Is he prepared to affirm or deny that God reveals himself to individuals and groups outside the church? Is he ready to work out the doctrinal position assumed in his answer? Is he prepared to bear the tension in church life between members who are suspicious of change and members who demand that the church should speak in the language of modern people?

How do we think theologically? The question gives rise to many other questions, such as, can there be scientific thinking or artistic thinking? Can a man's thinking be classified and described by a single label? What a scientist does when he is not doing scientific things is as important as what the artist does when he is not painting. A theologian is a better theologian if he is something of a scientist and something of an artist because his task is to be an expert in living rather than an expert in theology. Theology depends on science and art to bring hidden treasures to light. Scientists and artists should be depending on the theologian's belief that it is possible to make sense of human experience despite frequent evidence to the contrary. The theologian offers no quick way to attain the experience which includes all experiences and their interpretation; he should be stimulating us to seek the truth according to our particular work – the truth is one, but there are many paths which lead to it.

'My son, if thou come to serve the Lord, prepare thy soul for temptation. Set thy heart aright and constantly endure and make not haste in time of trouble.'* The theologian, like all other thinkers, is tempted to narrow human living in order to be soothing rather than truthful. He is tempted to make false simplifications; consciously he may withstand this urge but sometimes unconsciously he ignores or misinterprets known factors of a situation in order to comfort people. The theologian is called to expose people to the truth no matter what the result may be, and, what is more difficult, he must not tell lies to himself. Could it be said that for the thinker, theological or otherwise, courage is not so much a virtue as a necessity?

The church is short of clergy. Is the shortage of laity more serious? Is the shortage of lay theologians a serious handicap? Lay theologians, academic or non-academic, are usually free from the professional urge of clergy to explain and defend rather than affirm and rejoice. Always the church needs theologians who can expound the glory of living rather than sink into a bad church-centredness and/or something that might be called sacramental fundamentalism. Lay and clerical theologians have much to learn from one another about the nature of general theological thinking, and both have much to learn from all who, with them, are lovers of truth. It is not right to end with platitudes, so here is advice from the Book of Proverbs: 'The simple believeth every word: but the prudent man looketh well to his going'.**

* Ecclesiasticus 2.$^{1-2}$
** Proverbs 14.^{15}

THE BIRTH

The Nativity

In the beginning was the Word, and
the Word was with God, and the Word
was God. He was in the beginning
with God. All things were made
through Him; and without Him was not
anything made that was made. In
Him was life, and the life was the light
of men. The light shines in the darkness,
and the darkness has not overcome it . . .
The Word became flesh and dwelt among
us, full of grace and truth: we have
beheld his glory, glory as of the
only Son from the Father.

JOHN I 1-5, 14

And Joseph also went up from Galilee,
from the city of Nazareth, to Judaea,
the city of David, which is called
Bethlehem . . . And while they were
there, the time came for her to be
delivered. And she gave birth to
her first born son and wrapped him
in swaddling cloths, and laid him
in a manger because there was no
place for them in the inn.

LUKE 2 4, 6-7

God became man without ceasing to be God that men might
be godly without ceasing to be men. This is the mystery of the
infant in the manger, helpless and dependent upon a man and
a woman – Mary and Joseph.

There was no room in the inn; Bethlehem was packed for the
census. Each house was crammed and travellers were glad if

they had room enough to sleep in the open courtyard of the inn where the fire crackled and burned with bright flames. Without him there could have been no Bethlehem, no houses or streets, no inn, no power for authorities to summon people for the census. Without him there could be no expanse of sky and myriads of stars. Without him there could be no love of husband for wife, of parent for child, of friend for friend. Without him there could be no life, and yet we now look at him and see a new-born infant with all the appeal of a helpless baby.

We can never imagine a time when God was not, a time before time began. We never can imagine a time before the beginning when there was nothing, and yet we know that God is the maker of all things and of all people and that he made the substance out of which things and people are made. We do not speak of creation in the past tense because we are aware that new things are constantly being brought into existence. The birth of every baby is a profound change in the whole life of humanity and particularly in the lives of those most immediately connected with him. We know that our minds multiply thoughts endlessly and we are continually astonishing ourselves by the things which we bring into being so unexpectedly by what we say and what we do. Our very ability to grow and to find God in all things and all men has its origin in God who sustains and brings every mental activity to its fulfilment, provided that we do not check or distort the movement of our thoughts and wishes in a way of our own devising for our own power or comfort. Where there is submission to God there is the beginning of the adventure of finding truth and doing truth wherein human freedom grows.

We look at the little town of Bethlehem, its white buildings glinting in the moonlight and the dark countryside lying quiet around its borders. Town and countryside are both the creation of God, not made without him who now rests fragile and almost unprotected in his manger bed. It used to be thought that God could be found more easily in the country than in the town. But both country and town are expressions of his ceaseless creative activity, and further, town and country are also expressions of man's creative activity. Men shape the countryside by felling trees, draining swamps, quarrying rocks, planting crops and making roads and houses. None of these things could be done without the materials and the energy ceaselessly brought into being by God, who, at the very least, gives permission for man's use of things.

The building of towns and cities is as much the work of God as the making of the countryside. Men take dust and water and fire and out of these elements build the magnificence and complexity of towns and cities. It always causes wonder when we reflect on the mind and power of God who makes beings capable of such extraordinary work as that shown in the transformation of dust, water and fire into houses and streets. God is not only the source of the material substances necessary but also of the psychic energy which is necessary to maintain determination, imagination and active intelligence to devise plans and carry them out. When we look at a city we are moved to wonder and praise on account of the work that God works in men.

The life of a city is more than a marvel in bricks and mortar, for the human community that occupies the buildings of a city it is an expression of life that is quite remarkable for its degree of affection and tolerance. There is violence and vice and savagery in a city but not usually of such a quantity as to obscure the fact that a large community can live at close quarters without perishing through irritation, hatred and malice. The very existence of cities depends upon human beings' powers to submit to authority and to wield authority; without these powers there could be no community life, and God is the source of all power.

We look at the infant in the manger without whom no power could be. In his absolute power he now lies helpless in a town that could not be without him, set in a countryside that is also his under a starlit sky that could not move and live without his constant care. In spite of all this richness and all this wisdom he now lies in a borrowed bed content to make use of the stable because there is no room for him elsewhere.

The birth of our Lord always reminds us of the mystery of creation which is not a single act performed once and forever but the ceaseless activity in which man, the creature, participates in the ceaseless activity of God the creator. In fact each man has a responsibility for making himself and his fellows. This responsibility is consequent upon the fact that we are free to discover truth by our thoughts, words and deeds and what we discover enriches and expands our personality. This enrichment and expansion is not solely the possession of the individual, because the development of one individual affects others who in their turn affect him. We recognise the truth of this and we are aware of those people who affect us deeply by what they are, knowing that they have brought a part of us to life that might otherwise have remained undeveloped.

As we look at the stable and give our attention to the figures of the man and woman moved with reverence and wonder for the beginning of a new life we consider again the responsibility committed to them by this strange birth. We cannot plainly describe what is involved in this responsibility because we have to consider that he is both truly man and truly God. We do not know how developed a person truly man would be and have no way of describing the nature of his dependence upon others. We cannot attempt to speak plainly about one who is God and man but we can say that to be truly man must mean having the common experience of all men. All men need sleep and nourishment; they must learn to walk, to speak and to listen. They must discover to what extent the man must depend upon his fellows if he is to be a man and how much he must be independent of them if he is to develop his uniqueness as an individual. It will be sufficient to say that Mary and Joseph would discharge their responsibility for him by loving him constantly if we mean far more by love than sentimentality or possessiveness. When we speak of love for one another we mean primarily a reverence for the individuality of each person because each person is unlike anyone else and is destined to be himself most fully. Therefore love must respect the mystery of the beloved who has something to express with his life that no-one completely understands except God.

We picture Bethlehem silent and still as the night sky is slowly dispelled by the first rays of dawn. Gradually the light spreads until the darkness is completely done away and the new day begins. In the stable the new day shows him whom we call the Light of the World helpless and dependent on a man and a woman made by him who now depends on them.

The Shepherds

The Word became flesh, and dwelt
among us, full of grace and truth:
we have beheld his glory, glory
as of the only Son from the Father.

JOHN 1 14

And in that region there were
shepherds out in the field,
keeping watch over their flock
by night. And an angel of the
Lord appeared to them, and the
glory of the Lord shone around them,
and they were filled with fear.
And the angel said to them, 'Be
not afraid; for behold, I bring
you good news of a great joy which
will come to all the people; for to
you is born this day in the city
of David, a Saviour, who is Christ
the Lord. And this will be a sign
for you: you will find a babe
wrapped in swaddling cloths and
lying in a manger.'

LUKE 2 8-12

We picture the darkness of the stable broken by the light of a
single lamp, and in the pattern of darkness, light and shadow
we see the figure of Joseph, calm and protective, standing
silent and watchful. We picture Mary, whose anxiety, love and
wonder are expressed by her movement as she stoops to look at
her child. There in the stable would be the quiet that is made by
those who are giving attention to a being who attracts without
compelling and who makes the unquiet and disturbance of the
world seem transitory. We add to this picture the figures of the
shepherds. We are not told what they said, in fact we are not
told whether they said anything. It is most likely that they said
little. We can most easily picture them kneeling in adoration
before the manger that became a throne, made so by the King
of Kings. There are times when men can find no words to

express what they have to say and on those occasions silence is true eloquence and movement of the whole body takes the place of the rhythms and forms of speech. This is shown in the services of the church where worshippers have long since learned all that they could express by standing, by kneeling, by procession and genuflection. It is not that silent bodily movements can express all a worshipper has to say but that they make his worship more adequate by helping him to express that which lives and moves beyond the reach of words.

The shepherds left their flocks. They deserted their routine work on account of something that was much more important and which must be done at once. No doubt they were the sort of men who would make arrangements for the work to be done in their absence. Nevertheless, many might regard their behaviour as peculiar. Men should be dependable and reliable but there is something in human life which is not found and expressed by mere dependability and reliableness. We see this in those who protect themselves by the daily round of the common tasks which they allow to blind them from the call to unusual behaviour made to us by God, by others or by a prompter within us whose source we may hesitate to investigate. Perhaps the servant who buried his talent is a prototype for those who are determined to be dependable rather than run the risks that the maturity of love demands. There are times when the pile of dishes should remain unwashed, the house undusted, the beds unmade. There are times when heaps of paper must remain unfiled, routine letters unwritten, appointments cancelled. Happy is the man or woman who recognises the time to abandon ordinary obvious duties on account of unusual demands. This abandonment can cause misunderstanding and put others to trouble but there are things in life more important than the avoidance of giving inconvenience to others. There can be no list of such occasions, we can only hope that we may have grace and common sense to recognise them when we see them. Probably we equip ourselves to recognise these occasions by frequent meditation on the shepherds' readiness to abandon the usual for the unusual, but in saying this we bear in mind that works of mercy sometimes make the same demand on us as a call to worship does. This is so for the Christian because he realises that a work of mercy can be an act of worship if it is performed as a result of a loving disposition.

We picture the shepherds kneeling on the rough stable floor, and getting up to take their leave of Mary and Joseph. They would leave the darkness of the stable for the brightness of the stars and the quiet countryside. Thus they return to their work. The art of turning from work to worship and from worship back to work without making the worship mechanical or the work inefficient requires great flexibility of mind and attention. The shepherds had their walk across the fields as a time to prepare themselves for coming into Bethlehem and the walk back as a chance to prepare themselves for their usual work. In modern life we seem to have less and less time between happenings; because this is so part of the Christian discipline is to do all we can to acquire the flexibility to turn our attention from one occupation to another as quickly as possible.

After the departure of the shepherds we can imagine Mary and Joseph either talking about the strange happenings or thinking about them. Both would realise that the birth of this baby would be a changing point in their lives. They would know that a great deal depended on them for the development of the child who had become their responsibility. Parents are always aware that they cannot foresee the demands that children will make upon them as they grow up from childhood to maturity. No one can ever perceive how the interests and abilities of a child can lead him into occupations and friendships which his parents cannot and must not attempt to share. It is one thing to be brave about taking risks which mainly affect oneself; it is another matter to be brave enough to suffer others to run the risks which are part and parcel of their particular development. In the end good parents are those who know when not to interfere because they see clearly that each must lead his or her own life and that success in life does not mean avoiding danger and acting correctly. Fullness of life means the development of one's personality in association with others, caring for oneself because caring for others demands it.

In great joy and in deep sorrow we find it hard to get the words we want and sometimes we think that there are no words which will express what we want to say. On these wordless occasions our friends understand the meaning of our silence. In prayers we feel rightly that there are occasions when we don't know what words to use and trust ourselves to convey

our meaning in silence. Indeed there is no need to be
concerned about a prayer to which we can give no form in
words for God knows what we want to say more clearly than
we know. These thoughts become clearer in our minds as we
look again at the shepherds kneeling on the rough stable floor
and looking from them we see the still calm figure of Mary, and
Joseph motionless in his attention. This silence in the stable is as
typical of worship as the praise of the angels . . . 'Glory to God
in the Highest and on earth peace among men in whom he is
well pleased'.

The Wise Men

In the beginning was the Word, and the Word was with
God, and the Word was God. He was in the beginning with
God. All things were made through him; and without him
was not anything made that was made. In him was life, and
the life was the light of men. The light shines in the
darkness, and the darkness has not overcome it. There was a
man sent from God, whose name was John. He came for
testimony, to bear witness to the light, that all might believe
through him . . . The true light that enlightens every man
was coming into the world.

JOHN 1 1-7, 9

. . . and lo, the star which they had seen in the East, went
before them, till it came to rest over the place where the child
was. When they saw the star, they rejoiced exceedingly with
great joy; and going into the house they saw the child with
Mary his mother, and they fell down and worshipped him.
Then, opening their treasures, they offered him gifts, gold
and frankincense and myrrh.

MATTHEW 2 9-11

The story does not give any of the words used by the wise
men; the account of their actions does away with the necessity
of knowing what they said. They opened up their treasures,
'they offered unto him gifts, gold and frankincense and
myrrh'. Gold is the gift for a king and what gift better could be
offered to the King of Kings? Gold stands for purity and
regality. We can imagine Mary looking in wonder at the first
gift, not struck by its costliness but by its appropriateness. More
than any mother, and with more right than any mother, she
knew that her son was destined for greatness and the
unknown strangers expressed what she felt about her child.

We picture the second wise man kneeling to offer his gift of
frankincense, incense symbolic of the reverence due to him
who is born a child and yet a king, the Light of Lights,
begotten not made and yet found helpless babe. A person is
made great by what he magnifies; the worshipper is glorified
by the God he worships. The wise man's gift was an indication
that he thought this child's greatness would depend on whom

he worshipped.

The third wise man offered myrrh, myrrh to signify that greatness cannot be without pain and the king they want must be able to heal his own wounds if he is to be strong to heal the wounds of others. Myrrh also symbolises death because myrrh is used for embalming. The gift of myrrh makes the inevitable connection between the mystery of birth and the mystery of death. No doubt Mary made this connection when she watched the strange presentation. Every mother has pangs when she looks at the helpless infant in her arms remembering that he is mortal and will live and die in a world where sorrow and joy are strangely mixed in every movement of human life. Every mother remembers that her child will be caught up in the folly and savagery of a world where truth is always in danger of being mocked and justice prone to be scorned. Every time we think of the birth of Christ we find in our minds that the stable, his birth-place, leads us to look again at the cross where he died an outcast unwanted. But stable and cross lead us to look again at the supper table in the Upper Room and the broken tomb in the beginning of the new day.

The gift a person offers tells a lot about him. It is an exposure of what he thinks most necessary in life. Perhaps gold indicates that the first wise man considered that power, the power of a ruler, is the most important thing for the child before whom he bowed. We are often afraid of power but yet love without power would be unimaginable for love generates power. The second wise man by his gift indicates that the most important thing is to be at one with the source of all power and unashamed at the recognition of his own smallness and imperfection. We are sometimes in danger of adopting a pauper attitude towards God who wills that all things should be made ours by our use of them. In an attempt to counteract this pauperism we sometimes over-estimate the place of giving in our relationship with God. We know it is more blessed to give than to receive; what can we give that we have not first received? Love blurs the distinction between the actual giving and receiving and nowhere is this more clearly recognised than in the activities of our worship when we offer our gifts as the wise men did.

The third wise man did not deny the importance of power and being in touch with the source of all power. His gift of myrrh symbolised the place of compassion in the life of a powerful man. Whoever combines great power with deep compassion is a king among men wherever he is. The third wise man believed that the recipient of his gift was destined to express perfect power and perfect compassion in the pattern of his thoughts, words and deeds.

As we look at the wise men we are perhaps struck by the certainty and bravery they showed in giving up their work for an indefinite period to perform a task which so many of their contemporaries would describe as fantastic and would consider their quest as insane or irresponsible – people of education and position behaving in a way that seemed to deny both. Such a consideration helps us in our preparedness to answer unexpected calls to offer our gifts to the King of Kings by accepting the strangest tasks in the most unexpected circumstances. For some this may mean choice of the state of celibacy, for others the maintenance of a family household to enable its members to study, to pray and to work in such ways as their occupations demand. That is to say keeping a household so that a social worker, a teacher in school or a lecturer in the university, an artist or a civil servant will not be asked to conform to a family pattern that hampers them, but on the contrary recognising the mixture of solitude and company which each member needs, and an absence of disorder and chaos, while at the same time making sure that the discipline of the house has a positive concern for the development of each member.

The wise men came to do their homage later than the shepherds. The shepherds had not only the advantage of physical nearness but also that of growing up in a tradition that looked for the birth of the Lord of life and death when he came to deliver his own out of the bondage of sin and death and time. But the point is there is a difference between being late and too late. The wise men had a long journey to make, as far as actual distance goes. They had a longer journey to make in mind and spirit for they arrived at their destination by an unorthodox spiritual route. But all spiritual paths, when truthfully and honestly followed, give a knowledge of him who describes himself as the Way, the Truth and the Life. Without him there could be no thought, no mind, no decision, no adventure.

The blessing of the wise men's pilgrimage indicates the nature of our attitude to those who do not claim to be Christians but who diligently and courageously search for truth as scientists, scholars, philosophers, artists. To deny their significance would be to assume that nothing which is not specifically religious is of any account. The further assumption would be made that men could think and bring things into being without the power that God ceaselessly gives and without his initiation or even authority. Mary and Joseph recognised the wise men as strangers, indeed aliens, whose religion and culture had little or nothing to do with theirs. But Mary who accepted the angel's message and was ready to accept unknown shepherds as visitors, did not refuse the wise men an opportunity to worship the being without whom they could not be. For in him they lived and moved and had their being.

The Holy Innocents

In the beginning was the Word, and
the Word was with God, and the Word
was God . . . In him was life and the
life was the light of men. The
light shines in the darkness and
the darkness has not overcome it.

JOHN 1 1, 4-5

Then Herod, when he saw that he had been
tricked by the wise men, was in a furious
rage, and he sent and killed all the male
children in Bethlehem and in all that
region who were two years old and under,
according to the time which he had
ascertained from the wise men. Then was
fulfilled what was spoken by the prophet
Jeremiah, 'A voice was heard in Ramah,
wailing and loud lamentation'.

MATTHEW 2 16-18

The nativity stories bring certain sounds to our imagination.
When the Lord of life and death took our flesh upon him and
was born there was no fanfare of trumpets, no salute of guns.
His birth was heralded by his own small cry, the cry of a newly
born baby. We associate the sound of this small cry with the
song of the angels. But with these sounds there is the other
sound: the noise of weeping and lamentation of those who
would not be comforted. There is something profoundly
disturbing about tears which seem to be endless. We know that
then one cannot offer comfort but one can only weep with those
who weep. It is always a painful thing when grief and sorrow
are brought about by accident rather than through direct and
personal attack. The king had no direct quarrel with the parents
of the slaughtered children. His instructions to kill sprang from
his own fear of a possible rival in the birth of a child. Always in
life people suffer on account of the fears of others and no one is
a reliable ruler, priest, parent who is the slave of fear for himself
or for others. A sage said that the spiritual man's first duty is
the conquest of fear. Fear often leads to the use of the sword

and in this instance swords of Herod's soldiery flashed with
cruel purpose. The soldiers had no quarrel with the infants they
slew; they had no quarrel with the parents of their victims. They
were soldiers carrying out an order and their obedience led to
lamentations that ring in our ears every time we think of the
nativity stories in the New Testament. It is difficult to bear the
fact that the Innocent escaped at the expense of so many other
innocent children. Without this painful fact, and the other
painful facts of the Gospels we would be deprived of truthful
guidance about life which the Word made Flesh offers to all
who turn to him.

We are often bothered ourselves about the fact that in God's
world men are free to defraud, torture and kill their fellows.
Christians can bear this only by frequent reflection on the fact
that suffering and death are not the terrible things to God they
are to us. To think such thoughts is not to offer a defence of the
majesty and love of God. But nevertheless it is useful for us to
remember that there are happenings in life more terrible than
death and suffering, while there is nothing more true than that
in the best moments of our lives we should be preparing
ourselves for our own death and pain as well as making
ourselves ready for the death and possible agony of those
whom we love. Frequently in life we are disturbed both by acts
of direct personal venom and by the crushing force of
impersonal powers. This force is represented in the nativity
stories of the New Testament.

We have considered the soldiers carrying out their
instructions and cannot help hoping that in the use of the
swords they were unemotional. And we ask ourselves in the
long run which is the most pitiable – the bereaved parents, the
soldiers wielding their swords or the king who issued the
command for this systematic slaughter. The answer to this
question leads us to the mysteries of life and in particular to the
task of considering the extent of responsibility which each
human being has for his or her deeds. We have to go on to ask
ourselves, do we blame the soldiers either for being soldiers at
all, or for not refusing to obey instructions? We can only
speculate about what the soliders might have felt or might have
done. They represent for us all those who in the course of their
ordinary everyday life, are actively opposed to the reign of the
King who escaped the edge of the soldier's sword; and this is

no impersonal attack insofar as we feel the pressure of it in something of the way that Mary and Joseph must have felt when warned of the danger that threatened the helpless and innocent baby.

Herod and the soldiers represent for us all those who attack a spiritual power with weapons that can only be effective in the material sphere of life. To put this in another way, you may destroy a man but you cannot destroy the effect he has had, and will continue to have on others whether he be alive or dead. No human being can have a power to stamp a person out and make the future life be as if that person had never lived but their attempts to do so bring much misery and lamentation. At present in this country we are generally more aware of attacks made on us with the purpose of forcing us to lead a certain kind of life; not a religious or political kind of life but in general to be a consumer whose main occupation is concerned in having sufficient money to spend on the goods which are made to appear attractive and necessary for the happiness of life. In short it is constantly suggested that fulness of life consists in abundance of possessions.

Herod set out to kill a rival: the one he believed to be his enemy was not his rival nor anyone's rival. He taught us that each man is unique and therefore need not rival anyone or fear rivalry. Nevertheless when a man sets out to develop his particular talents with the single mindedness of a Christian loving God he invariably finds opposition. This opposition is often strong in those who love him best and demands of him a certain ruthlessness if he is not to become a conformist whose one concern is to fit in with other people in all circumstances. In developing himself he becomes aware of the extent of the enrichment brought about by association with others who are as anxious as he is to reverence the unique in others and in themselves. The unique is often heralded by small unobtrusive things like the cry of a newly born infant but sometimes it seems to be greeted by the song of the angels. These triumphant signs do not mean that the sound of mourning has died away. In life knowledge brings both joy and sorrow as one finds in society the contemporary equivalent not only of shepherds and wise men but also of Herod who sent his soldiers to encircle the crib with drawn swords.

The Presentation in the Temple

In the beginning was the Word, and
the Word was with God, and the Word
was God. He was in the beginning
with God. All things were made
through him; and without him was not
anything made that was made . . . And
the Word became flesh and dwelt
among us, full of grace and truth;
we have beheld his glory, glory as
of the only Son from the Father.

JOHN 1 1-3, 14

And when the time came for their
purification according to the law of
Moses, they brought him up to
Jerusalem to present him to the Lord . . .
and to offer a sacrifice . . . Now there
was a man in Jerusalem whose name was
Simeon . . . Inspired by the Spirit he
came into the temple; and when the
parents brought in the child Jesus,
to do for him according to the custom
of the law, he took him up in his arms
and blessed God . . .

LUKE 2 22, 24, 25, 27-28

We can imagine the small child being put into the arms of the
old man. The eyes of the old man by the light in them gave an
indication of the many things he had seen and read. We
probably imagine his face wrinkled deeply giving trace of
former concentration on thought and work. Special lines about
his eyes would indicate that he had smiled at much in spite of
all the burdens and dangers of living through days of unrest,
surliness and latent hostility. Perhaps we imagine that his voice
was gentle and clear as we look at him lifting his eyes from the
child to the mother of the child and saying to her "Behold, this
child is set for the fall and rising of many in Israel and for a sign
that is spoken against (and a sword will pierce through your
own soul also)". Did she wince at these words? Did she look

tremblingly at her child or did she look at the old man with
bewilderment in her gaze? Or was there no surprise in her face
because Simeon had put into words what she had been
thinking?

A woman knows that her baby will suffer if he loves much
and will bring others suffering too. She will ponder Simeon's
words concerning the downfall and rising up of people as a
result of the life of her child . . . He came to his own and his own
received him not . . . as many as received him to them gave he
power to be the sons of God. Absolute truth incarnate attracts
or revolts men; confronted with truth there can be no neutrality,
it is a case of either accepting or rejecting in whatever form
rejection takes. For Christians the Cross is the symbol of a
human rejection of truth incarnate. Every baby born causes
profound changes in the whole of humanity and particularly in
the lives of those who are immediately associated. Every
mother realises the responsibility that will belong to her new-
born baby as he grows and develops but it is only one mother
who has ever felt that her baby's life would bring about such
changes in time and in eternity, for all men live by him and
through him.

'and a sword will pierce through
your own soul also'.

Mary would be torn asunder by conflict; a conflict brought
about by a desire for her son's safety and a desire for his
greatness. She would want to protect him from all that would
harm him and this would conflict with her desire to expose him
to the perils of loving truth and doing truth. She would know
the common weakness of wanting her child to remain a child
and wanting him to become a man in whom she would take
pride even if his manhood meant loneliness and pain for her.
All parents realise sooner or later that the child who is so
helpless and so dependent on them must grow to be a man and
that in this development become a stranger in his own house.
The love that held him close to them is also a means of
separation, for love makes people mature and in maturity
uniqueness of the individual comes to life and power. Thus
there is always a human loneliness which is never completely
overcome by association with human beings; it is only in God

that this loneliness first becomes tolerable and finally acceptable as an inevitable experience in the development of men and women.

Simeon knew much of the agony that Mary might expect. He knew that she would be one of those who either rose or fell in response to the life of her son on earth. He knew that this child would disturb fear and even anger in the hearts of women whose sons would leave home to be with him. He would not be scornful, we may think, but would be gentle in his thought about them because sometimes the intensity of love heightens the perplexity of a woman divided between her approval of her son's adventure and disappointment in losing him from the family household. No doubt it would be in Simeon's mind that parents find it hard to accept that when their children leave them it is a sign of good parenthood and a recognition that it is important to have a good home to leave.

THE LIFE

Gospel Images and Life Today

'He was in the world, and the world was
made through him, yet the world knew
him not. He came to his own . . .'

JOHN 1 10-11

God became man without ceasing to be God,
that men might be godly without ceasing
to be men.

ST. ANSELM

He was in the world, the world was made by him, and the
world knew him not. He came into the world he had never left.
The world was not new and strange to him; he knew it but it
did not know him. The maker of all was not recognised by
those he made. In him was life, and the life was the light of
men. The brightness of his light was as darkness; men looked
at him and turned away to the little lights kindled by their
understanding and imagination. The most godlike gifts can
sometimes provide us with the opportunities for behaving in a
most ungodly way. Often what some of us call our goodness is
more alarming than what we call our sins. There is a type of
goodness which neither recognises the holiness of the saint nor
the evil of the very wicked.

He came unto his own . . . He came, his words often seemed
riddles and his actions as bewildering as what he said. It was
not intelligence that his audiences lacked. Some of the good
people of his day were not brought up to be capable of
recognising righteousness when expressed in unconventional
ways, just as people of these islands used to confuse
conventional respectability for Christian righteousness. It takes
a certain amount of greatness in a man to recognise greatness
in others; it is only by God and through God that a man can
know God. God became man without ceasing to be God that
men might be godly without ceasing to be men.

He came . . . the Gospels proclaim the wonder and the
bewilderment of his coming. Wherever he went he claimed

attention by his presence. At first sight he appeared to his contemporaries as merely another rabbi with his pupils tramping the countryside living sparsely on the small alms of Galilean villagers. The majority of his contemporaries came into no direct or indirect contact with him, at least not to their conscious knowledge. Of the people who met him, none could be neutral – they either received him or rejected him. To receive him did not mean that they fully understood him. Admiration is never dependent on knowledge but it cannot survive without evidence capable of examination. In our own reading of the Gospels we can sometimes sense through our experience how apostles, pharisees, sadducees and the common people regarded him as incalculable. The Fourth Gospel gives us the image of him as the Good Shepherd and as the man with a scourge in his hands before whom the money-changers and the merchants fled. The same Gospel gives us the image of him as the wedding guest, as the figure dressed as a slave, carrying a basin of water and a towel in the upper room. We are shown him as the exhausted prisoner privately examined by the Roman governor while the crowd outside shuffled and murmured. We cannot for long forget the figure of the crucified Lord of life and death, and the soldiers shaking dice at his feet with his clothes the prize for the winner. And that image must always be side by side with the image of him breaking bread with his friends on the night he was betrayed and with the image of him standing beside the open tomb.

No single Gospel image will satisfy us. For example, reflection on him as the Good Shepherd emphasises the gentleness of his care for people while the man with the scourge emphasises his readiness to oppose those he loved. Both such elements are difficult to combine in a single image. The generous provider of wine stresses a part of his ministry which is difficult, at the beginning, to reconcile with the man blessing the Cup at supper using the strange words 'This is my blood which is shed for you . . .' We could put images aside and look at his words. We could reflect on the Beatitudes, the Lament over Jerusalem, the Seven Woes. We could study the parables again and again; but whether we study his words or reflect on the gospel images of him we can never discover one simple saying that satisfies as complete knowledge of him. No statement in words is adequate and no single image or combination of images will do. There will always be times when we know the need of going through the words that describe him and the images that portray him into a wordless adoration of him who is all in all, in whom all fullness dwells, who calls us to the life outside our body's walls and beyond the frontiers of our present knowledge. He is in the eyes that see, in the object seen and in the mind's desire to understand; he remains with us in our fragmentary understanding – without him we can do nothing and be nothing. We can look for him in the ordinary things of everyday. Every small thing, a pebble or a blade of grass, can be our entry into the mystery of the whole universe. God is in all things and all things are in him but mere examination of things is not enough; we have to examine them through him who called himself the way, the truth and the life. We do not find him by ignoring the things he is continually making but through use of all he makes. We search for his pathway at the highest point of creation which we know is in the realm of human relationships. But the use of 'search' and 'look' in this connection is misleading. We cannot, as it were, step outside the network of our relationships and make notes; we are not spectators but participants who share in the ceaseless movement of human relationships. We could perhaps be better advised to talk about extending our awareness of what is happening to us and through us.

God became man without ceasing to be God that men might be godly without ceasing to be men. 'Have this mind among yourselves, which you have in Christ Jesus, taking the form of a servant, being born in the likeness of men. And being found in human form . . . became obedient unto death, even death on a Cross.' (Philippians 2) He was obedient even unto death. He submitted to the conditions which inevitably led to his arrest and execution. He did not invent a type of life which could be lived in society without touching the depths of people's being. For instance, the washing of the disciples' feet was the performance of a task, a necessary task, which had been omitted. He supplied the omission. We submit to the social conditions of our day, for submission is the first step towards their modification and our fulfilment of ourselves. We can only pray and think and work as men and women of the twentieth century in a community where the scope of our significant activity is small. Nowadays a Good Samaritan does not tend the injured man; he dials 999 and takes care not to touch the injured one for fear of causing further trouble to what might be a broken limb. Such action is small, if actions can be measured, but a human action gets its significance from its necessity and appropriateness not from the cost to the agent or the worth of the benefit conferred on others. A full human life can be lived in the most obscure and out of the way places. On the first Palm Sunday it was not at the gates of Rome that our Lord wept but at the gates of Jerusalem; Jerusalem, the capital of a little-known province on the fringes of the Empire far from the centre of civilisation.

Do the Gospel deeds and you will know the Gospel truths. Religion is not learned, it is practised; the learning is in the doing but the doing is not a copying of anyone else's life but a living of one's own life. Our Lord tells us to affirm ourselves; to fight for our liberty and to maintain our personality. This is expressed in these injunctions: 'Thou shalt love the Lord thy God . . . Thou shalt love thy neighbour as thyself.' 'A new commandment I give unto you, that ye love one another; even as I have loved you, that ye also love one another. By this shall men know that ye are my disciples, if ye love one another.' Love God: love your neighbour: love yourself. Love one another the way Christ loves each of us and all of us together. To love yourself is to be free through serving God whom to serve is to reign, thus liberty and personality are preserved. To love others as our Lord loves us is to live and act in such a way that their liberty and personality are enhanced. That is, I am to reverence my brother's personality as much as I reverence my own. St. Paul puts it this way: '. . . I say, through the grace given me, to every man that is among you, not to think of himself more highly than he ought to think . . .' A man is to think highly of himself but not more highly than he should. Love of neighbours, love of God and love of self are all expressed in the style of life lived by a man who thinks highly of himself.

A man has a right to think highly of himself because every man born is given the status of being human. Without earning it, he is given the power to bring new things into being. Everyone born is called, through his birth, to participate in God's ceaseless creative activity. We do not, as it were, stand

before God as paupers, orphans, toadies or criminals but as
beings who fail to do things great enough to be commensurate
with their status of being human in the world God loves and
which we are called to love the way he loves it. Not that love of
this sort means acquiescence. Godly love leads a man to criticise
and to oppose those whom he loves just as he continues to love
those who oppose him. This must be put in simple concrete
terms because this love of the world has to be concerned with
men and women, and men and women as they are divided into
groups, governments, trades unions, universities etc. There is
a worldly way of life expressed in many forms, some noble,
some trivial, and there will always be tension between those
who lead the godly life and those who lead the worldly life.
Our behaviour, as Christians, will often appear deceitful to
ourselves and to others. Life is such that often a Christian finds
refreshment, excitement and a reverence for truth and justice
among worldly friends that contrasts oddly with the timidity
and insipidity of many of his fellow Christians. Sometimes
Christians are conscious that secular papers are more religious
and adult than various church papers. This kind of experience
goes to show that the best church members are those who best
appreciate the good lives and works of people whom we
describe here as worldly. Not only that, the best church
members have always been her most keen and well-informed
critics.

Any reflection on the Gospels and their imagery ends by
leading us to a consideration of the activity of God working in
us and through us now and our failure to read our present
situation and discover the one great act which would be an
adequate response to the voice of God in social changes. Side
by side with that we remember that our reflection on the Gospel
images leaves us with no single image of our Lord which can
satisfy us, nor will the whole constellation of them express the
truth which is in him. We rejoice in these images and perhaps
our rejoicing is greatest when we are beyond them in the light
that is too bright for a man to see much. Similarly we rejoice in
the manifold signs of God in the social achievements and
revolutions of our day and perhaps we most greatly rejoice in
the works of men when we see beyond them and their works
the greatness of him without whom nothing is made that is
made. Contemplation of the city landscape with its sky-

scrapers, electric coolers, factory chimneys, church towers and steeples can be ways of entering into the ultimate mystery of man in God and God in man and of God in the world and the world in God. This mystery requires image after image, concept after concept, as we grope for ways of explaining to ourselves the nature of our relationship between one another in God and through God. In the end we know that living is more important than thinking and that our actions are ways of getting to know the world and men and God in the unity of living.

PRIORITIES

He came to his own home . . .

We picture to ourselves the dying fire in the Inn's courtyard,
the huddled forms of men sleeping round it. We hear the
sound of those talking late, children murmuring in their sleep
and the crackling noises of the fire. In the stable little can be
seen; the lamp is small, there is just light enough from it to
break up the immediate darkness . . . a little light surrounded
by darkness . . . we hear the cry of the newly born baby; there is
no guard of honour, no fanfare of trumpets. Absolute power
needs no setting, no pomp. Absolute power transformed the
stable into a palace and the manger into a throne. He came.
There are no clever things about his coming; we are relieved,
the light shines in the darkness enabling us to make sense of
life by living it. Life is not to be thought about but lived, and the
reason, the hope, the faith and the love will be truly ours when
we cease to regard them not as possessions but as parts of our
being, shaping all we do and expressed through all we do. We
are human and human beings become clumsy, confused and
alarmed from time to time, and again and again we have to
rediscover what is ours through the birth of a baby – born a
babe and yet a king.

'He came unto his own . . .' He had to come at a particular
time, to a particular place to particular people. In becoming
man there could be no other way; he could not come to all men
in every place at the same time. He had to submit to the human
limitations of time and space. The taking of our manhood was a
real taking. He participated in the social conditions as they
were. He did not seem interested in social reforms as a modern
philanthropist might be. He did not set out to alter the social
order, he conquered by submitting to it. Submission is always
one of the measures of human greatness. The wise mother
accepts the facts of her case – her poverty, the ability, or lack of
ability, in her family and brings them up accordingly. The fact
that our Lord was brought up in a carpenter's household in an
obscure town shows that circumstances are not all that matters
in our life work of being human. A man can be human
anywhere at any point in history as long as he submits to his
conditions, not passively but creatively as an artist might if the

only materials available for him were a piece of paper and a bit of charcoal.

Sometimes Christians are concerned by the seeming unfairness of his coming to one particular generation and so giving it more chance of salvation than other generations. We are always living in two spheres of existence, the temporal and the eternal. In the temporal we are limited by the boundaries of time and distance. In the eternal we are not so limited. We experience at least a foretaste of the eternal sphere whenever we realize that we do not live within our body's walls and whenever we realize that the chronological order of events is not a pattern we can impose on the most important of our experiences. For example, again and again we discover the falsity of the chess-board view of life. This is the view that human beings live in a pattern of thought, decision, overt action, reflection on action taken . . . whereas our most important actions are done without the opportunity of preparatory thinking and the making of a formal decision to act in a certain way; we only discover what led us to act after the performance of the act. Perhaps it is that the temporal should be described as all that has to do with clocks, diaries, calendars, plans for houses to be built, banking accounts, card indices and the like, all drawn up and obeyed promptly and efficiently. Perhaps the eternal is to be described as the sphere of living where a man's occupation is not of first importance, where he cannot find words to say what he wants to say, where time is not measured by clock, diary or calendar, where events do not seem separate and are yet coherent whether regarded separately or in their totality, where the distance between people is made short by love and long by hate.

That last paragraph was an attempt to describe the kind of experience of the temporal and eternal which indicates that it does not matter when our Lord came to his own . . . for all generations are contemporary with him. He could have come to men of any race or culture with equal chance of being recognised, for all are his own – no place could be unfamiliar to him and no men strangers to him. But a choice was made, a people were prepared specially over centuries of hardship, made his own in a special way, and the majority did not recognise him but as many as did recognise him became fully alive.

He came unto his own, he came into the world he made and never leaves. He is our Saviour and our Judge; he could not be the one without being the other: this enables us to bear the thought of the day when we shall know as we are known. In the meantime he comes to his own in devious ways. His is the bread of life we break and share, his is the cup we bless and take. His is the word that is spoken. His is the sorrow of those who are lonely and forlorn on account of their love of him and of their fellows. There are few human ordeals more difficult to bear than love which is denied adequate expression in overt acts. His is the joy of all who exult in the glory of life here and hereafter. He comes to his own . . . his own are not all behind ecclesiastical walls. Some of them are bewildered both by the world and the church in their love of truth, which prevents their ease in either world or church. Some are tortured with the inability to be content because they cannot be sure that they know. Others of his own do reverence to him in the laboratory where accuracy can be a petition, and joy in discovery an act of praise. Others find him (whether they recognise him or not) in their use of words or in their delight in colour and form. In our day many of the things Christians value find their custodianship not in ecclesiastical but secular circles. The great truth that men have a destiny which cannot be described in moral terms or in terms of helping one another, the attempts to make a coherent description of modern spirituality, the effort to unravel the tangles made by those who hate city life together with all modern life, are all things which receive more attention from those other than churchmen. The church has so long been occupied with morals and practical social work that the new mind, the new learning and the new behaviour have largely shaped themselves outside ecclesiastical spheres. The church's occupation with morals and social works was highly necessary, if overdone by some, at the point where the bulk of the population was illiterate, ill-fed and ill-housed and where the country's prosperity was won at that price. That necessary work has come to an end and the church's work in the community, pastorally, is concerned with the recognition of the modern mentality and spirituality and a sociological study to discover who are the poor; and perhaps they are the spiritually poor – the people who dare not stop to think.

The Lord does not live and work in his church alone. But if

people want to find him – or rather come to him – they must come to the church. No matter how indifferent, apathetic and insipid church members may be they cannot quench the lamp of truth which dimly shines on in such surroundings. When he came to his own, he took our flesh upon him and submitted to the limitations of humanity. Now the church is his human agent, not his only agent, but his chief agent. He has not conferred sinlessness upon her members. She has her terrible moments when members are obsessed with trivialities as well as her great moments when the place in which she worships becomes alive with the Presence of God in the Bread broken and the Word spoken.

ACCEPTANCE

'He came to his own home and his own people received him not. But to all who received him . . . He gave power to become children of God.' (JOHN 1 11-12) '. . . to all who received him . . .' Numbers of people did not receive him but welcomed an idea of him formed partly in reaction to the power of his presence.

We picture him surrounded by the Galilean crowds; men pressing forward so as to catch every word he said and to see the expressions on his face. The gospels say that the common people heard him gladly. In Marxist language – the proletariat heard him gladly. They were bitter; they were angry and frustrated on account of much unemployment and of the prosperity enjoyed by Sadducees under the hated Roman dominance. They were at one with the rest of the nation in condemning the tax-gatherers as traitors earning their money from the enemy. The common people had nothing to lose and everything to gain in an attempt to free the nation from Rome and in the consequent alteration in the national social structure. The common people welcomed our Lord in the hope that he might be the leader to bring them out of the present captivity. When they looked at him they only saw in him the picture of the man they wanted him to be. Many people with power over a crowd accept the role which the crowd gives and play the part the crowd requires while using the crowd's support to achieve ends hidden from the crowd who listen, applaud and cheer wildly. The gospels indicate that the crowd diminished in size when people saw that he did not conform to their idea of him. The gospels draw attention to the savage attack made on him in Nazareth, to the murmurings in the synagogue in Capernaum, to the roar of the crowd rising up from the packed street outside Pilate's palace: Crucify him!

The Pharisees would have accepted our Lord on their own terms. They would approve if he were content to accept the role of reformer and revivalist. It would be commendable, in their minds, if he worked to keep the religion of the fathers unaltered and to build up national unity and patience so that the little nation might outlive the mighty Rome. In doing this they would expect him to use his influence in Galilee to keep

the Zealots from attempting any further rising (their last
outbreak had had tragic results). As a group they would not
accept him. And this group contained the most religious and
the most devout people of the day. The group failed to
recognise him not so much on account of their sinfulness but
because of what they would call their goodness. Sometimes
what a man calls his goodness is more alarming and shocking
than what he confesses as his sins.

He was accepted by individual Pharisees who were glad to
have him as a guest in their houses. Perhaps the modern
parallel to this is found in those who are actively making their
homes not only moral but religious. These same people in their
public life, work, recreations, conform to popular notions of
behaviour as distinct from Christian notions. For these people
church, school, and university are judged in the benefits they
confer on family life. The family is mysterious, wonderful,
beautiful, but whenever it is made the first loyalty of life it is no
longer beautiful but a prison. No full human life is lived entirely
within the walls of a house. All of us have known, and know,
great families; we also know men and women who foreswore
family life in response to other calls.

Our Lord dined with Pharisees; he also dined with publicans
and sinners. He was on easy terms with so many of them that
he was called 'the friend of publicans and sinners'. The sneer
carried with it a political attack as well as questioning his moral
and religious seriousness. To be a publican or a sinner was not
one of the necessary qualifications required for friendship with
our Lord. Mary Magdalene was not just any sinner, nor Levi
and Zaccheus average publicans. Each of them had something
in them that is best called innocency. None of them desired to
be taken for better people than they were; they were not
hypocrites. There seems to be an innocency shared by the saints
and the very wicked. There is a clue for the reason of this in the
beautitude: Blessed are the pure in heart for they shall see God.
Blessed are the single-minded for they shall know God. It
seems that a single-minded evil person arrives at a certain
clarity of perception which the saint is given in his different
journeying. The hypocrite, as typified by the Pharisees of the
Gospels, is so occupied in giving an imitation of being holy
that he dismisses any experience if it spoils the role he is
playing. So it is with hypocrites in a fantasy world of

their own, finding in it those who are ready to co-operate with
them in preserving the fantasy. The hypocrite must go on
playing his role. The Christian church has always had a
responsibility for hypocrites and a missionary urge to deliver
them out of their world, out of the prison of fantasy. Logical
arguments, abuse, scorn do not go deep enough: in the end
grace is the thing which opens the door to free the captive
hypocrite. But this belief calls for activity by all who take part in
a mission to hypocrites. The fundamental movement of this
activity lies in the recognition of the spiritual dangers incurred
by all who recognise their mission in life. In opposing the
enemies of truth one is in danger of becoming false. You
become like that to which you pay most attention, whether you
disapprove of it or approve of it. The truth of this spiritual law
becomes clearer in reflection on our Lord's interview with
Pilate. Our Lord said to Pilate 'If my kingdom were of this
world then would my servants fight . . .' If our Lord had
opposed Pilate directly, even in this interview, he would have
lost his identity and be found playing a role such as that
suggested by the expectations of the common people. It is a
curious spiritual fact that affection for others must always have
an element of non-engagement, an element which seems like
aloofness.

Individual Pharisees, members of the common people
(sociologists would use this label as convenient for indicating
this social group within the nation), certain sinners accepted
our Lord up to a point. The Gospels show him as courteous and
good-humoured with them. For the most part he made no
great demand on them. These relationships, of course, were
completely different from those made with the men who
answered his call to discipleship. Of these men he made the
most exacting demands; as their association with him
developed they saw more and more how exacting these
demands were. Those who observed would note superficially
that here was a small group of disciples tramping the
countryside with their rabbi. There were many such groups
and contemporary people would not consider this mode of life
unusual; the unusual would appear when the stories of his
execution and the empty tomb began to be fairly widely
known.

The disciples are described by our Lord as those who

continued with him in his temptations. The Gospels leave us images of them; the chief images are for most of us connected with their joining him in the Upper Room, running from him in the garden, meeting him again in the Upper Room on the evening of Easter day. What sort of men were they? They gave up all for him. They gave up money, position and ease to be with him. They did not choose him; he chose them. He called, they answered. In the present habit of mind, one asks 'What were their qualifications?' The fourth gospel says that they believed on his name. This was more than a formal assent; it was a recognition of truth incarnate by men innocent enough to know the truth. In saying this it should be reflected that the innocence of grown men is different from the innocence of childhood. Children have an innocence that owes much to ignorance and inexperience. The innocence of a grown man consists in his habitual entry into activities and relationships with no thought of his immediate, or future, gain in doing so. The innocent man is not the sinless man. In the Sermon on the Mount figure of speech, he is the good tree that beareth good fruit. The good tree has bad fruit from time to time, but year by year its total crop is good. 'By their fruits ye shall know them'; but that does not mean that the judgement could be made by the deliberate selection of untypical examples.

In any age the qualifications for discipleship can only be expressed in the most general terms. A disciple is one who is fulfilling his vocation to be human in the only way it can be fulfilled which is through being a member of the church. To talk of qualifications in connection with discipleship is always misleading for qualifications do not consist of a completed thing to which you can point. Qualifications are rather an element in your living than a possession to be guarded; they are always in the process of being made. Ultimately we are led to the truth that God qualifies those whom he calls through their living out their response to his calling. God calls us now as ever; that is, he does not call us by special means of communication but rather by established ways – by the combination of happenings in the physical universe and in the realms of human relationships which go to make up the situation in which we live and move and have our being, and that situation is as surely in God as God is in it.

REJECTION

He was in the world, and the world was
made through him, yet the world knew him not. He
came to his own home, and his own people received him
not.

JOHN 1 10-11

And when he drew near and saw the city he
wept over it, saying, 'Would that even today you knew
the things that make for peace!'

LUKE 19 41

The things concerning him had a purpose, something other
than people in the city longed for.

Pilate waited nervously. Roman governors were always
uneasy as Jewish feasts drew near. Excitement and political
fervour were mixed up with the devotion of the pious.
Anything could happen, the population of the city was
temporarily trebled at the time of a feast and the near shoulder
of the Mount of Olives was covered with small tents. Crowds
thronged the city streets and in the Temple enclosure the Court
of the Gentiles was packed . . . and a Roman sentry paced his
beat on the top of the courtyard's broad wall.

The Jewish authorities were also nervous. The unknown
Galilean had become both a political and religious danger; they
would not feel safe until he was silenced. There was only one
way to do that, as Caiaphas the high priest pointed out to the
Council. After discussion went on for some time he brought it
to an end by saying that if the death of one man meant the
political safety of the nation that man must die. The Council
knew what that entailed. His assassination could not be
considered; the Jewish Law Court could not pass a capital
sentence, therefore he must be charged at the Roman Court
with a political crime. The Council dispersed, no doubt leaving
the matter in the hands of a few.

Our Lord came to the city presenting a riddle in his person
which his contemporaries found unanswerable. He fitted into
no category, he could not be classified. At a time of political
tension this was dangerous. He certainly could not be called a
Sadducee by birth, upbringing or inclination. The Sadducees

consisted of a small group of wealthy and powerful families. The High Priest was always a Sadducee and his office was as if, in English terms, he held at the same time the responsibility and power of both the Archbishop of Canterbury and the Prime Minister. The Romans, as their way was, allowed the Jewish nation a certain clearly defined autonomy. They were content that the government of the country should be in the hands of the High Priest and the Jewish Council. Taxes must be paid, riots avoided and a limited jurisdiction observed. A fairly strong Roman garrison was maintained as a constant reminder of limited Jewish power and as a warning of what Roman legions could do if peace were broken. The Sadducees hated the Romans, but the existing arrangement suited them for the time and guaranteed them their continued wealth, power and prestige. If they hated the Romans they despised the Pharisees. The Pharisees were the steady hard working middle-class, merchants, shop-keepers, traders and farmers. They contained within their numbers some of the most devoutly religious people and were as intensely patriotic as the Sadducees. They would agree with them that this was no time for any violent attempt to drive the Roman legions out. Not so many years earlier the Zealots had fought a brief and pathetic guerilla battle which was no more than an irritation to the Romans who, in punishment, burned some half a dozen Galilean villages and deported numbers of men to be slaves. The Pharisees and Sadducees for political, religious and utilitarian reasons believed that the future lay, not in military measures but in patient acceptance of Roman rule; then they, as a nation, would outlive the Roman Empire. To achieve this Sadducees and Pharisees held that it was necessary to maintain national solidarity. Anyone who did anything to endanger this national unity was to be condemned both on patriotic and religious grounds. The whole political-religious situation can be seen in one single instance such as this – 'Do you keep the Sabbath?' was for some both a religious and political test question; for some only a political test.

Our Lord certainly did not come to Jerusalem as a Sadducee. He did not say 'I am of the Pharisees' or 'I am a Zealot'. The Pharisees could have recognized him if he had been a zealous conventional religious teacher and they would have welcomed him. The common people would have continued their support if he had accepted the role of the popular leader of a revolt. Each group waited . . . puzzled. He addressed none of them formally, as far as we know, but there were certain signs which could not easily be read. One of the twelve disciples was a Zealot, one was a tax-gatherer; that is a naive patriot and a traitor earning his living by working for Rome. Individual Pharisees were glad to entertain him; the common people heard him gladly and he was known to be the friend of publicans and sinners. He did not set out to be cleverly ambiguous. It was his desire to be precise which others found so confusing. He had to show himself as neither ignoring nor giving full approval to the groups in the society of his day. His power lay not in allegiance to any of them but in the maintenance of his distinctness from all of them. His view of the things that belonged to the peace of Jerusalem was shared by no one, not even his disciples and supporters. He came to the city gates surrounded by the cheering crowd, but he was as alone there as he was in the Garden when the disciples slept for sorrow. At least a few knew later how he felt because the gospel says when he saw the city he wept over it.

He has left for us a vivid example of what happens when all press us to take a definite stand on the issues that really count. There is the way of yielding, the way of evasion or what looks like quibbling. The church is urged to speak out clearly; individual Christians are asked for definite opinions. Most of this pressure is from within the church. There is also a certain amount of this demand for exactness made by those who can only maintain their stability by attacks on established institutions. In effect people say 'What has the church to say about nuclear disarmament, comprehensive schools, family planning, trades unions, prostitution, capital punishment, racial inequality, juvenile delinquency, universities for all, capitalism?' There is a question about right and wrong in all these things which religious people say they know; why do they not speak out? Few will wait long enough for the answer. Christians cannot give unqualified approval or disapproval any more than they can claim, by their faith, to have sufficient knowledge to prescribe a cure for juvenile delinquency or homosexuality. Christians must say that the modern world has gone mad on cures where there can only be endurance, and that this craze has led people to look for infallibility where it

cannot be. Our basic fact in matters of human behaviour is that
human beings are to be reverenced, in other words they are to
be given the best conditions we can make for the opportunity to
fulfill their vocation to be human. They are not to be protected,
pampered or debased by sadism or love turned into a
possessiveness which makes a prison. It is easy to say what
should not be done but the great positive human actions
depend on the agent's discovery through understanding his
fellows in the situation, or in the spontaneity which is made
possible by his habitual style of life, a style of life in which the
performance of the act and the discovery of the necessity of the
act are simultaneous.

Inevitably positive living brings church and churchmen
where they must set out to speak clearly about the great human
themes of love, hate, death, birth, treachery in the light of
eternal truth and the immediate temporal situation. What we
have to say is usually misunderstood or found unintelligible.
This is particularly true in our society in which there is a sharp
division between those who hold that there can be a literal
description of reality which indicates a man's correct action in a
given circumstance, and those who hold that there cannot be a
literal description of reality and every act of man's is an
exploration of reality. Thus we hold that human acts are not to
be written off as correct or incorrect, or as moral or immoral, but
as attempts to express love by beings whose power does not
depend on knowledge possessed but on the certain hope that
the genuineness of the love ensures the reality of the action.
Had our Lord and Pilate met in this generation our Lord might
have said to him 'My kingdom is not of this world, if it were,
then would my servants reason, prove, command and exert
influence through the use of modern publicity methods at
whatever financial cost. But my kingdom is not of this
world . . .' As then, so now this would have hurried the
interview. In the end words are only words. Our Lord stepped
out of the Judgement Hall on to the raised platform outside it.
The crowd became silent and intent . . . until a murmur
gathered speed and volume, 'Crucify! Crucify! Crucify! Away
with him! Away with him! Barabbas! Barabbas! We want
Barabbas! We want Barabbas! We want Barabbas! Barabbas!
Barabbas! We want Barabbas!' People could understand
Barabbas. The High Priest and the Jewish statesmen felt that

they could handle anything that might arise through Barabbas being free. But this other, there could be no guarantee for what might happen if he were free. He stood there, the prisoner at the bar, alone in the face of a hostile crowd, as alone then as he was on the first Palm Sunday when he saw the city and wept for it. Tears only are only tears if they are instead of action or the painful alternative, the acceptance that no action is possible; the guilt, the injustice, the lie have their hour and their power.

He came to his own and his own received him not. The place of his rejection had to be the city which both he and his enemies loved.

'WE HAVE BEHELD HIS GLORY'

The disciples did not behold his glory as spectators; they enjoyed it as participants in it. To see is to share and to share is to be fundamentally altered. His glory is ours because we are his and he is ours; what happens in his life affects our life; what happens in our life is initiated by him in such delicate movement that the process cannot be subjected to analysis. We do not recognise the moment of its beginning, much less its power and illumination within us, though we do recognise thoughts, words and deeds which seems too great to be of our making and yet more ours than anything else we do. Sometimes we are aware of a state of being which is incapable of verbal description and does not lead directly into action but we know that we will, from that moment, think and act in a new way. We must not seek this experience directly nor look on it as a reward or the inevitable result of hard work. The great things in life happen to us by a seeming effortlessness, but it is the hardest work in the world to preserve this effortlessness. The work consists in the cutting down of mental and physical work in the way that the Sermon on the Mount implies in the injunction: 'Seek ye first his kingdom and his righteousness and all these things shall be added unto you.' This is not an injunction to pious idleness and to occupying oneself entirely in undefined work with spiritual things. It is to do one's best to occupy oneself with securing the necessities for physical life here in the middle of one's more serious occupation in all that is concerned with the fulfilling of the vocation to be human. It is not to labour for the meat that perisheth and not to be anxious; it is wishing to be alive rather than happy; it is to admit that much of what we do is beyond our understanding and out of our control; it is to know that peace is often no more than a brief assurance that you are living on the right lines. To keep us from becoming like angels we are to pray 'give us this day our daily bread.' Man does not live by bread alone, but he cannot live without it here. There is something bad whenever an individual or community becomes obsessed with the importance of sufficient bread. It is the human glory that we can recognise that there are more serious things in life than being hungry. It is the human glory that we have discovered that no one is fully living until there is something for which he is prepared to die. These things can be said and done because we both beheld and behold his glory in one another and through one another. His glory makes all little human scrambles for safety and understandable goals look pathetic. A man swims best when he is out of his depth; a man lives best when he is beyond his understanding.

'We have beheld his glory.' His glory was not expressed in laying his hands on little children and blessing or in healing the sick and teaching the ignorant. If there were no children to bless, and no sick to heal and no ignorant to teach, his ministry would still have been effective. Church people are often perturbed because the state looks after the education of children and adults, as well as providing hospitals for the sick. As for our Lord, so also for his church; the church's ministry to the world does not consist merely in performing deeds of mercy. Our Lord did not seek crucifixion as a good thing in itself; he accepted crucifixion because it was inevitable in the circumstances of his ministry. Church members now are called to maintain their integrity in the face of apathy; it is always a test to keep integrity when no one directly attacks you. The church and its members must learn, in every generation, not to judge their devotedness by the acuteness or nature of the suffering borne. The test of the church's life is in terms of its relevance rather than the number and character of its martyrs. The worship of the church is an act in time which is concerned with eternity; worship is an act performed in and out of time. The church's mission to the world is also an act performed in and out of time but if the act is to be a real act it must be intelligible to those who pay attention to it. Preaching is to be addressed to the preacher's own generation; pastoral and evangelistic work are to be informed through a compassion which rejoices with all that is good in that generation as well as feeling the sorrow and shame. The churchman is to love the world as much as he loves the church and the church as much as he loves the world. He must love God more than either church or world because he loves each for God's sake.

In every generation there is to be a magnificence about church life – its buildings, its liturgy, its preaching; and pastoral care and evangelistic concerns should all combine to express the mystery which we are all caught up in. The manner in which officiant and congregation act, apart from words

used, is the fundamental element of all Christian worship, and
naturally so because dance is the oldest art. One could say that a
deaf person ought to be drawn into the movement of worship
by the movements of his fellow worshippers. This is as true of a
large church where there is room for the use of ceremonial as it
is of a small building where movement is curtailed. The manner
in which people enter church, the way they stand to sing
hymns, their bodily stillness during prayers, their repose in
listening to scriptures and sermon, their demeanour as they
approach the altar – these bare and simple movements are as
much a part of worship as the words used. It is not that there
should be a self-conscious study of simple necessary
movements in church such as standing, walking, kneeling, but
that there should be much reflection on the majesty of God and
the greatness bestowed on all who worship him. Such
reflection will tend to express itself in the gait and will move
people to consider more precisely what they are doing when
they worship him who became man without ceasing to be God
that men might be godly without ceasing to be men. Worship
is one of the ways of being godly, and the manner of those who
worship is not only an expression of their devoutness but also
helps to create the atmosphere which makes worship possible.
This manner has a great deal to do with the dignity and
compassion of Christians, ordained and lay, in the expression
of their pastoral and evangelistic concern for men and women.
For we approach all people with a certain reverence; not only
are they made in the image of God but God himself stirs within
them; without him they could not exist, but because he is in
them even their degradations can neither make them
contemptible nor alter our connection with them and our
responsibility for them.

We have beheld his glory: that is, we share in it, and so it is a
way of saying that we realise the importance and meaning
which he gives us, individually and corporately. We may echo
his own words as given in the Fourth Gospel – if we had not
known his glory and the meaning and importance he gives us
we would not know sin, but now we have no cloak for our sins.
But he is just and righteous, forgiving the sins of those who
turn to him. We are to be penitent before him and we are to bear
our penitance with dignity because we are given power to be
the sons of God. We, therefore, do not justify ourselves before

men but we proclaim the sovereignty of God by our manner, our words and our deeds both in specifically religious circumstances and in conditions which are not so. We must use every means in our power to stretch people's minds to be aware of happenings which cannot be described in terms of family life, nor ecclesiastical life in the narrow sense, nor as intellectual, but rather in terms of an experience of the Holy calling us to our mission in life, that is, to be what no one else can be, and by being what we are, express our worship of Almighty God and our concern to draw others out of the whirligig of nothingness into the way of life. We are not to force others openly or set out to coerce them in hiddenness. We are to believe in the attractive power of our mission; we are to believe in it even when we are in our worst moods, or when men of character and prestige turn their backs on us, or because we are startlingly aware of our unworthiness. We are given a mission, we are given sufficient knowledge and adorned with sufficient greatness to fulfil our mission through living in the name of our Lord. We are to be clothed with greatness, as the Lord of life and death allowed himself to be dressed up with a purple robe and a crown of thorns before a crowd that mocked. He did not lose his dignity but his tormentors lost theirs; which leads to the reflection that whenever you submit others to indignities you diminish your own dignity. Dignity is far from being a matter of self-concern but only has reality in our dealings with one another, and never can be attained if sought as an end in itself. Great people are not aware of their dignity but others become aware of a great person's dignity by their reactions to his presence.

In modern society we enjoy pomp of all sorts – the Royal Family, the Trooping of the Colour, Cup Finals at Wembley, the Opening of Parliament, the arrival, activities and departures of film stars. We enjoy pomp and ceremony, but dignity makes a good many of us nervous of presumptuous behaviour in others and in ourselves. Dignity is difficult in a period such as ours because it only grows easily in a stable society living on traditional cultural patterns. Churchmen are therefore called to live with dignity, with more than a touch of greatness on account of the stability of the church and its traditional behaviour patterns though, of course, these must be unravelled and re-woven generation by generation.

The first disciples beheld his glory in the breaking of bread, in the chains that bound him, in the scourge lifted to strike him, in the cross made to humiliate and destroy him and in the tomb that could not hold him. We do not spend the whole of life attempting to re-live these happenings though our living depends on them. We behold him here and now within us calling us to take up the cross of discipleship and wear the crown and cloak, sure of the blessed hope of wearing the crown that fadeth not away. He teaches us to think and act victoriously before the battle is more than half begun.

MEDITATIONS ON THE TEMPTATIONS
AND PASSION OF OUR LORD

Behold, my servant shall deal wisely,
He shall be exalted and lifted up,
And shall be very high.
Like as many were astonished at him,
(His visage was so marred more than any man,
And his form more than the sons of men),
So shall he sprinkle many nations;
Kings shall shut their mouths at him,
For that which had not been told them shall they see;
And that which they had not heard shall they understand.

We have not an high priest that cannot be touched with the
feeling of our infirmities: but one that hath been in all points
tempted like as we are, yet without sin.

Therefore let us also, seeing we are compassed about with so
great a cloud of witnesses, lay aside every weight, and the
sin which doth so easily beset us, and let us run with patience
the race that is set before us, looking unto Jesus the author
and perfecter of our faith, who for the joy that was set before
him endured the cross, despising shame, and hath sat down
at the right hand of the throne of God.

TEMPTATION (1)

MATTHEW 4 1-11; LUKE 4 1-13

The silence of a mountain top can be peaceful the way the
silence of a house on an early summer morning can be
peaceful. The silence of a mountain top can also be full of
threats the way an isolated house after midnight in the depth of
winter can be full of threats for the sleepless. A person at peace
welcomes the silence of mountain top or house; a person at war
with himself finds that silence outside him sharpens the conflict
within him. Without sufficient solitude there can be little
strength; without solitude the internal conflict deadens a man
by using up so much of his energy that memory,
determination, imagination are distorted and flounder in
confusion. Men and women are drawn to the person who is at
ease with them because he is at ease with himself when he is

alone. To be at ease with yourself is to give yourself over to
your highest ambitions without caring about your safety. In life
there is nothing more dangerous than acting to secure your
safety; you must run both the risk of society and the risk of
solitude; faith gives us boldness to banish caution. This
banishing demands different things from different people.
Some should live more of their lives in the company of others;
the greater number should live more of their lives in solitude,
that is to say not in perpetual solitude but by deliberately
planning to have frequent short intervals of solitude between
the other activities of life. This is not selfish; in solitude love
grows, love of God and love of others. Love can only develop
in truth, and truth can be painful; truth can only develop in
love, and love leads us into the resolute action to which truth
points.

We picture to ourselves a bare mountain top, its outline
jagged and forbidding against the clear hard sky. The last
couple of hundred feet rise sharply and here there might be
some protection from the sun among a few bare rocks. We
picture the relentless sun by day and the intense cold at night.
Far below the mountain top we see villages and towns as small
as children's toys. Occasionally there is the swift movement of a
bird in flight; nothing else interrupts the stillness.

We look at a solitary figure on the mountain top. His face is
set in thought, his body is still, absolutely still. He is not
looking at the jagged outline of the mountain top against the
sky; he is not looking at the plains spread out below, he is
giving his attention to another scene. We are looking at him in
the moment between his baptism and the beginning of his
ministry, we are looking at him in the moment when the whole
course of his ministry was clearly determined. Thoughts begun
in the carpenter's shop were developed to sharpen his
determination and give it the right means of expression. We
see him at the point where he is making his plans for the
beginning of his work. We look at him – he is motionless but
not tense, his body's poise shows something of the nature of
his occupation.

Planning always brings pain and the realization of further
pain to be borne if the plans are to be brought to life. In
determination to do the right the strongest temptation to do
the wrong becomes forceful and clear to the thinker. 'If thou be

the Son of God, command this stone that it be made bread.' The bread could be broken and given to the multitudes and the multitudes would look to him as the giver of bread. After all would it not be best to take away all the anxiety born of poverty and to free the poor from their obsessions? The hungry cannot see the truth, the anxious can have no peace. 'Command this stone that it be made bread.' People will understand the giver of bread, people will understand plans to remove the conditions which form their prison. How can a man be free when he is shackled with poverty? Do conditions foster a man's distress? Does human distress persist in spite of or because of conditions? He would not be concerned so much with arguments as with people: children, listless in their movements through lack of sufficient food; women grown hard-faced and bitter-tongued in their constant anxiety to provide enough food; men sullen and weary, waiting in the market-place, cursing themselves, cursing everybody for the absence of work and of wages. The faces of people in their quick changes of expression are more eloquent than the ablest of arguments. He could never forget the faces of the poor; the faces of the rich would be just as clear in his mind: the face of the rich man's daughter as she laughed at beggars squabbling over a coin tossed in their direction; the face of the rich man when the narrowness of the street forces him to walk too close to someone who is dirty in the sad way that the destitute are dirty; the face of the cunning man lurking in the shadows, eyes alight with greed and expectancy. 'Command this stone that it be made bread.' Destroy a source of temptation which is too strong for both rich and poor, destroy that source of temptation and make people ready to hear and receive truth. Too much bread, too little bread are both conditions which overpower men, for men are weak and to love them is to remember their weakness. The faces of people who have no worry over food and the faces of people who do not take pride in being without worry over food are more human than the faces of the supercilious and the cringing.

'Command this stone that it be made bread.' Go to the multitudes as the provider of bread first, then later you may become more than that to them; people will be grateful if you set out to feed them. Human beings are on their guard when anyone threatens to destroy their responsibility by a gift that is too large and immediate. To be responsible is to have meaning, to have the mark of being an individual; an unwise gift, or a heavy bribe disguised as a gift, makes an attack on fundamental human responsibility. It is more characteristic of love to share than to give. The picture for the love of the Lord is not that of the extravagant, lavish, careless benefactor. The picture for the love of the Lord is that of a friend with his friends at the supper table: as we look we see that he is taking bread and breaking it and giving it to them; for us the picture speaks of far more than the sharing of bread; every meal is more than that. The significance of this particular meal is clearer for us when we look again at the mountain top and see the solitary figure whose stillness of body showed something of the nature of the occupation of his mind. Listen to words that describe his conflict: 'If Thou be the Son of God, command this stone that it be made bread . . . Man shall not live by bread alone, but by every word of God.' Every word is a deed, every deed is a word – the broken bread at the supper table speaks of the sharing that is characteristic of the love that is ready to share all with all.

TEMPTATION (2)

MATTHEW 4 1-11; LUKE 4 1-13

To be alone is to think of many things and to see many things – to be alone often requires bravery, for in solitude the mind's best deeds are performed in the face of an advancing, encircling opposition within the mind itself. The mind is not like a debating-society; the mind is an arena in which there is endless movement, endless struggle and where peace is only given through the movement and the struggle. 'Then the devil leaveth him, and, behold, angels came and ministered unto him.' The peace of God is freely given, but it is to be freely received for it is given neither as a right nor as a reward.

We are looking at a solitary figure on the mountain-top; to look at him is to remember that all things were made by him, and without him was not anything made that was made. He has all to give and now he is concerned with the manner of the giving, rather he is concerned with the nature of giving and receiving; in love the distinction between giving and receiving is blurred, for sharing provides the true way to think of love.

'And the devil, taking him up into an high mountain, showed unto him all the kingdoms of the world in a moment of time. And the devil said unto him, All this power will I give thee, and the glory of them.' People would fight bitterly over bread, they would keep it from one another, they would buy it and sell it . . . some would eat too much, some too little, some would not eat at all. The way people behave about bread shows their weakness, their distrust of one another, their greed in the present, their fears for the future. To control may well be the surest expression of compassion. Rule people for their own good; minimize their terrifying power of choice . . . in the end they will learn to love the Ruler on account of the benefits of his rule, they will see his wisdom and his mercy in every regulation that he enforces for their well-being. The only freedom human beings can have is in knowing that they can have none.

'All this power will I give thee . . .' The ruler shows power; to be powerful is to show yourself capable of great love; no one respects love without power, people need first and foremost to be assured of strength and then they will love the strong man. People want to be protected most of all from themselves because they are afraid both of their highest ambitions and of their basest desires. They keep themselves ignorant of these fears, they are also terrified of inability to recognize what is wise and true and good. A display of competent strength puts people at their ease and inclines them to accept the most severe rules as amiable advice given by an equal. The most powerful demand is the concealed demand; when it is effectively made people give you everything and they think that in doing so they have conferred a favour on the giver. Rule – in your strength support their weakness. Rule – what they would not do of their own accord, they will do at your behest as long as you make it appear that they have made the choice themselves. There are more ways than one of subduing the obstinate by power – power in the end is everything, men will do nearly anything for power, let them all have power, but, of course, you will see to it that they do not abuse it and that would be the supreme act of love.

Our most common temptation is to do what is blatantly the wrong thing. Sometimes, and this is a mark of the goodness that is in us, we are tempted to do the right thing in the wrong way. We are, for example, tempted to make a parade of our humility to influence someone who has given himself over to pride. When we look at the solitary figure on the mountain-top, we can only imagine that his temptations were something like the temptations of our best moments – the moments when we are tempted to do the right things in the wrong way. This is a clumsy and inadequate way of talking, but love for him and reverence for him call us to understand him as best we may in the light of faith and revelation. Understanding begins in faith and ends in love; in love there is always the urge to understand the beloved and the realization that full understanding eludes us. We must not avoid looking at him and thinking of him in case we come to false conclusions about him; what we do in love, he will correct in mercy.

As we think of him we would get lost in the maze of our thinking if we did not look again and again at the happenings which give rise to our thoughts about him. At a particular point in time temptations took concrete definite shape in his mind, and once they took concrete shape in his mind they gathered in power as all temptations do whenever they are organized and given a body. Hidden events of the mind have a distinct importance which is made plain by subsequent events in the exterior visible world. The connection between events gives them place and significance in love; the inner events and the exterior events when coherently woven together make the totality of life, but one of the signs of sin is incoherency, the incoherency of events disconnected or falsely connected. His temptations were events which did not happen outside his control but which rose almost directly from his steady control of himself – the person with a diffuse mind, unsteady in all its workings, is capable neither of fixed determination nor of great temptation.

So he refused to use power to enfeeble men and women in the name of love. A refusal is only in part described as an attitude – the attitude must be expressed in acts which are appropriate to it. We are given a glimpse of the inner struggle in which the attitude was set, we are given many glimpses of the actions by which the attitude was maintained. Look at him now wearily following Pilate into the judgment hall for the second of two private interviews; in the street outside is the crowd swaying and craning their necks to watch what is happening, there is the murmur of many voices and the noise of harsh laughter; the high priests look at one another as much as to say 'Just a matter of time now'. The door of the judgment hall closes, and the judge is alone with the prisoner. 'Art thou the King of the Jews?' and Jesus answers him, 'Sayest thou this thing of thyself, or did others tell it thee of me?' Pilate answers 'Am I a Jew? Thine own nation and the chief priests delivered thee unto me: what hast thou done?' Jesus answers, 'My kingdom is not of this world: if my kingdom were of this world, then would my servants fight, that I should not be delivered to the Jews . . .'. Outside the crowd shuffle and shout and jostle one another impatiently. The chief priests look at one another as much as to say 'This must be nearly the end'; and so it is . . . the door opens and Pilate appears, his face set hard as if to make compensation for the uncertain light in his eyes and the difficulty he has in keeping his mouth firmly set. The crowd become silent and tense. Pilate begins, 'I find in him no fault at all. But ye have a custom, that I should release unto you one at the passover: will ye therefore that I release unto you the King of the Jews?' The last few words of the sentence are lost in the crowd's roar 'Not this man, but Barabbas'.

'All this power will I give . . . Rule them for their own good, protect them from their weakness and sinfulness.' 'Barabbas! Barabbas! Barabbas!' roared the crowd. Here is the mystery of absolute power; here is the mystery of submission, and victory through submission in a strange conflict where victory and defeat are lost sight of by Absolute Love who can only think of sharing guilt and glory.

TEMPTATION (3)

MATTHEW 4 1-11; LUKE 4 1-13

From the mountain-top towns and villages could be seen in the
distance. In every village, in every town there are people whose
feet have become weary through the repetition of the same
short journeys day by day; there are people whose hands are
weary through the repetition of the same task again and again.
The lives of many people are colourless and drab. Is it their
occupations that make them colourless and drab, or do people
make their occupations look like themselves, that is, like the
preoccupations of their mind? Is weariness sometimes the
expression of a spiritual state just as drabness may be? Let us
leave these questions to turn our attention to the solitary figure
on the mountain-top. In his solitude he is aware of the people
he has come to save, just as much as he would be whenever he
moved among them in the narrow streets of the towns and
villages that were just within the range of his vision from the
mountain. He would not so much reason about them as think
of them. The man who had married young and who had lived
all his life in the same little village, saying the same things day
after day to the same people at the same time; the woman who
knew what her husband would say on all occasions; the boys
and girls who were just old enough to feel they were to be
denied the freedom once longed for by their parents who had
now forgotten even the longing. He would know that for
many, sensation, interest and excitement seem to be more
necessary than bread. If people cannot do sensational things
themselves they can live on the seansational things that others
do. After all perhaps people at first need the strengthening
power of excitement to lift them out of the routine habits of
thought and action which are stifling them and blinding them.
Such thoughts as these may help us to see the force of the
temptation portrayed in the picture of him for a moment poised
on the battlement of the tower, the crowd below stock still,
paralysed with excited fear . . . one tense moment and then a
piercing scream. But the picture is not to be taken at its face
value; it is the mind's pictorial way of saying 'Why not draw
people to you by miracle?' People long for the extraordinary,
the sensational, the unique. A unique mission might well be

started by a unique happening, and even maintained by unique happenings. We think like this because in thinking of him we want to understand his temptations; to understand them more clearly is to see his purpose and his glory, just as contemplation of his purpose and his glory sooner or later shows something of the nature of his temptations. We think like this because we have sometimes, perhaps often, longed for the sensational, the stirring, the adventuresome. Adventure, like truth, resists the greedy searcher; adventure, like happiness, is only found when you are looking for something else. That something else must be so big, so compelling, that the adventure is accepted as inevitable and never regarded as standing on its own merits.

The highest adventures are often feats performed in solitude. We are now looking at our Lord as he accepts the full purpose and burden of his work and at the same time hardens the opposition within himself to its fulfilment; for every determination to do the good brings to life a fresh temptation to do the evil. In temptation we are often provided with a parody of the good we would do. In our Lord's interior struggle he had to live with three false images of his Messiahship: the provider of bread, the benign ruler, the wonder worker. Use bread as an inducement, a bribe; use bread as a bribe and a weapon; no one will recognize that you have turned it into a bribe or a weapon. Rule people for their own good. The use of power is the surest expression of love. The use of bread and the use of power might look like coercion and corruption, but could anything be more innocent than the use of sensation? No one has any material gain in such a use. They expect, some of them, that the Messiah will suddenly appear in his Temple, this combination of sensational happening and traditional expectation would commend itself – most of the devout are simple people, and with the simple much is excusable, much understandable.

The end does not justify the means; the means must proclaim the end. It was right that he should draw all men to him, and to use a phrase like that is to speak of real activity on his part. But what was that activity to be? There were three false images of it and there was one true image. The nature of that true image is manifest in his every deed and word.

Look again at the figure poised on the battlements of the

Temple tower; look at the crowds below, transfixed, breathless. A moment of tension, a scream, and the noisy acclamation of miracle. Think of all this image implies – someone whose life had nothing to do with reality, whose actions were no more than exciting irrelevant scribblings in the margin of a book. Look at that same figure, his head and his shoulders just visible over the heads of the crowd; they are shouting at him, but he is too weak to reply, even if he would. The nails in the wood are holding him fast. Listen to what they are shouting 'save thyself, and come down from the Cross'. 'He saved others; himself he cannot save.' 'Let Christ the King of Israel descend now from the Cross, that we may see and believe.' What sensation could never do, submission accomplished. 'He was in the world, and the world was made by him, and the world knew him not.' But he knew the world and loved the world. 'Save thyself and come down from the Cross', some spat as they shouted. This defeat is his triumph; we are looking not at the victim but at the victor. The first movements of the triumph were made on the bare mountain-top; the moment of the mountain-top and the moment of the crucifixion may have been widely separated when measured by time; but they were close together in the way that is not measurable by clock or calendar.

THE MOVEMENT OF THE PASSION

MATTHEW 27; MARK 15; LUKE 23

To look at the passion of our Lord is like looking into a mirror and seeing yourself. To look at the passion of our Lord is to contemplate its movements: the palm-strewn road twisting through the cheering crowd; the uproar in the Court of the Gentiles, the crash of tables overturned; the hands taking and breaking bread, the hands receiving the broken bread; the hands giving silver coins, and the hands receiving silver coins in the lamplight; the patterns made by the shadows of olive trees on the ground of the moonlit garden; the flash of swords, the closing circle of armed men; the firelight in the dark courtyard, the crowing of a cock; the roar of the crowd, the choice of Barabbas; Pilate with basin and towel washing his hands; the hiss of the scourge through the air; the clanging of hammers; the searing pain, the emptiness, the loneliness, the darkness, the whole world staggering and reeling in his feebleness; the strange triumphant cry; the departure of the sightseers, the scoffers, the soldiers – three empty crosses left standing in the silence; the fragrant garden at dawn where a woman weeps.

To look at the passion of our Lord is like looking into a mirror and seeing yourself, for it shows you what you long to be and what you are; it shows you your despair and your hope and the power of God. To look at the passion of our Lord is to contemplate its movements: they tore down branches from the palm trees and flung their cloaks on the dusty road; someone bled his fingers in breaking a branch from a thorn bush and shaping it into a crown; they broke a tree and made it into a cross. The tree they killed became the tree of life, for it bore the Lord of life in the bitter moments of his glorification.

To look at the passion of our Lord shows you how to set about being what you long to be. Evil can be overcome, but only with good; being good is not a state but a process and the process is sometimes hardly distinguishable from pain but the pain is preferred to escape from the struggle; such is the wisdom of love.

To look at the passion of our Lord is to see among its movements the figure of one dressed like a slave moving with towel and basin and the figure of one dressed in the robe of a judge taking towel and basin and washing his hands. The one performed an act for others, the other acted for himself. 'If I wash thee not, thou hast no part with me.' 'I am innocent of the blood of this just person: see ye to it.' 'I depracate this action and I dissociate myself . . .' One washing cleansed, the other made the stains deeper; both washings in their different ways proclaimed association.

To look at the passion of our Lord is to see among its movements the haggard look on the face of Judas as he carries the bag with the thirty pieces of silver in it back to the priests; it is also to see the contempt and loathing on their faces. 'I have sinned in that I have betrayed the innocent blood.' And they said 'What is that to us? See thou to that.'

To look at the passion of our Lord is to see that we can neither proclaim our innocence, after the fashion of Pilate, nor make use of the fruits of treachery, like the priests, without sharing the traitor's guilt. There is only one thing we can do; we know what that one thing is when we look at the figure dressed like a slave and at the same figure stripped of his clothing to be made ready for the crucifying.

To look at the passion is to see that we are not spectators but participants, for in it there is a reiteration of his words 'If any man will come after me, let him deny himself, and take up his cross daily, and follow me'. 'Let him deny himself', and let him 'take up his cross daily' – both phrases imply concrete action. The bearing of a cross also implies that there is a place of crucifixion, which means that there is also a place of resurrection. For us there are the equivalents of the crowd that shouted 'Hosannah!' and the crowd that roared 'Away with him! Away with him!' There are also the equivalents of Pilate who feared the results of honesty and Judas who could not bear the results of treachery. But the passion is not only a manifestation of the powers of darkness; darkness cannot swallow up light. At the moment when all men seem against you and your defeat almost accomplished, that is also the moment when you find that you are not alone and what looked, at first, like the signs of defeat are the beginnings of victory, rather a sharing of the strange victory first proclaimed through the signs to be seen in a fragrant garden at dawn.

THE BREAKING OF BREAD (1)

MATTHEW 26 26-29; MARK 14 22-25; LUKE 22 19-20

'In the same night that he was betrayed he took bread and when he had given thanks, he broke it . . .'

By that time, silence was possessing the city; the narrow streets were full of shadows, the buildings cold, white and still in the moonlight. Somewhere the high priests waited apprehensively for what might happen, they hoped for the fulfilment of treachery. In the governor's palace Pilate knew the restless anxiety that was always his torture at the time of a feast, 'There must be no upheaval, no riot, no bloodshed, except the blood I shed'. His hopes always were placed in what others might do or in an uneasy reliance on his own sense of the expedient, his quickness to recognize the safest course.

'In the same night that he was betrayed.' It was a tense night for many, but for the multitude it looked exactly like scores and scores of other nights: the narrow streets full of shadows; the houses cold, white and still in the moonlight, here and there the dim figures of men and women moving in and out of the shadows and disappearing; the noise of barking dogs and the sound of voices rising and falling in the quiet of the night.

'In the same night that he was betrayed.' There was quiet in the Upper Room, attention without anxiety; hope made fear bearable, trust made hope possible, this present moment was a healing one for all – delivering each from the dread of the power of the past and from the dread of the power of the future. In turning their eyes to him, they forgot themselves and so had peace in him; confidence is not made, it is found and it can only be found in him. He knew the traitor's intention and his motive; he knew the course that events must take, for events were in his power. 'There must be no upheaval, no riot, no blood shed except my blood.' Life can only be brought forth by life; the beginning of life was in God, the renewal of life must also be in God. What he makes, only he can remake. None can create life but God and only he can re-create.

'In the same night that he was betrayed he took bread.' The hands that took the bread were rough strong hands, hands made powerful by heavy manual labour; the hands were powerful, the fingers were the virile flexible fingers of the craftsman who is accustomed to delicate accurate work. As a carpenter he bought wood in the form of living trees; these were felled and the carpenter saw to it that planks were made smooth and to the length and thickness convenient for his immediate tasks. Trees were thus transformed into ploughs, into yokes to harness oxen, into tables, cupboards; trees were transformed so that their part in the daily lives of people was changed. The tree that swayed in the wind while its leaves sang the song of the wind became a plough to till the ground and thus part of the source of food. Food is more than the sustenance of life – food, when shared, is a means of transforming acquaintanceship into friendship. To break a loaf and share it is to do something you could not do with words, just as bringing a person to your house to sit at your table is to do something you could not do with words. What is already formed we transform by our use. The tree must be broken before the plough can be made, before the table can be made. The loaf must be broken before it can be shared – every use of the table is a further transformation of the tree, every use made of the scraps broken from the loaf is a further transformation of the loaf. A tree does not go on being a tree for ever, but its life goes on in different forms; a loaf does not go on being a loaf for ever, but its life goes on in different forms. At the very centre of our religion there are scraps of broken bread reminding us that in the creation of God there is endless formation and transformation; that everything formed is split in pieces and each piece split, and every splitting is the beginning of a new form of life.

'In the same night that he was betrayed he took bread and when he had given thanks, he broke it.' He transformed, in breaking, what was always formed. Continually we take what has already been formed and transform it, breaking the formed thing up into new sources of life. We take the tree and make the table, we take the table and use it for many purposes; we take the toil of the silkworm and, weaving it, break what we have woven into many forms of many colours grave and gay.

'He took bread.' We take what we find already formed: he took the bread he had formed and transformed it; he, the source of all that is, took common bread and remade it into something most uncommon. Often at mealtimes he did what he did that night; that is to say, he took the loaf and gave thanks, and broke it and gave each a scrap of the broken loaf. He continually used a loaf to make and maintain an intimacy between himself and the disciples, he continually used bread to make many things that were not bread, but which could only have their origin in bread and in the use of bread. Bread, ultimately, is made through the action of wind and sun and rain on first the seed and then the shoot springing up out of the brown earth. The force that drives the clouds and generates the power of the sun is the energy of God. Bread is a form of the divine energy, this form of the divine energy can be used to bring into being the power of affection. A loaf shared draws people together; in such a statement a loaf is the name of the many transformations that happen when the loaf is shared in love. Often he had broken bread with them. You can imagine how they felt whenever he sat with them. You can imagine how they felt that night he was betrayed. What they felt did not matter, what he did was of supreme importance. Whenever he spoke, he spoke with power, his words were deeds that accomplished transformations. The night that he was betrayed there was something he could not do with words, something he could only do by taking bread and breaking it. What he did that night is not over and done with; what he did that night is not shut within a particular place nor closed within one short hour. Physically every act, such as the breaking of bread, sets in motion a series of physical changes which will not come to an end till the end of the world. Within every hour that people spend with one another there are happenings which alter the whole life of those who are together, and that alteration does not stop at a boundary mark. Every transformation in a single human life causes changes throughout the whole human family – the words whispered to a friend in private are spoken to the whole of humanity.

The smallest acts produce a complexity of results and series upon series of results beyond our prediction or control. 'The same night that he was betrayed, he took bread.' The hands that took the bread were the same hands that so often took wood and fashioned it into what it had no power to be apart from him. He took bread and by breaking it fashioned it to become that which it could not be apart from him. The hands that so often took the wood were the same hands that made the wood; the hands that took the bread were the hands that made the bread. Not many hours later men broke those hands with the nails they drove through them to hold him helpless on the tree which they had taken and twisted and broken and shaped into the form of a Cross; they deformed what he had formed, in the hope that they could destroy what was beyond the power of their hands. The hands they broke and fastened to the tree were the hands that broke the bread; they were also the hands that broke open the tomb that could not hold him. The broken tomb cries aloud the endlessness of all he ever said or did on earth; it cries aloud that he who had no beginning could have no end. The broken victorious hands are more than strong enough to draw us into the endless present that is the eternal Now of God.

THE BREAKING OF BREAD (2)

MATTHEW 26 26-29; MARK 14 22-25; LUKE 22 19-20

'In the same night that he was betrayed he took bread and
broke it.' He said to Judas: 'What thou doest, do quickly!' The
evils that develop in a period of hesitation are manifold, these
particular evils are prevented from multiplying by the decision
to do the evil deed. 'What thou doest, do quickly!' The words
brought the hesitation of Judas to an end . . . he moved to the
door, pushed it open; for one moment darkness met light on
the threshold, Judas closed the door and went into the
darkness, down into the street filled with shadows; he moved,
a dark figure in the moonlight, and sometimes a shadow
within the shadows. 'What thou doest, do quickly!' 'Be brief,
what have you to tell us?' The priests' manner would be curt,
no one cares for a traitor, even those who benefit from his
treachery. 'What have you to tell us?' There would be no
friendly response evident in the faces of those who listened,
merely a hardness of the line of the mouth, the eyes glittering
coldly. 'He took bread and broke it.' The priest took a bag and
opened it carefully and began to count. He gave a scrap of
bread to each; the silver in the priest's hand shone brightly in
the lamplight and clinked discordantly. 'When I sent you forth
without purse, and wallet and shoes, lacked ye any thing? And
they said, Nothing. And he said unto them, But now, he that
hath a purse, let him take it.' The priests kept their bargain,
they counted thirty pieces of silver into Judas's hands, the
current price of a slave in the market. 'Now you know what you
are to do.' Judas knew, but his mind was a whirl of broken
images, mad images that tore and tormented him in their
movement. 'He that hath no sword, let him sell his garment,
and buy one. For I say unto you, that this that is written must be
accomplished in me, And he was reckoned among the
transgressors: for the things concerning me have an end.' The
disciples said 'Lord, here are two swords'. One can almost hear
his sigh. The appearance of the traitor, the glint of swords by
moonlight, the roar of the crowd, the hiss of the scourge, the
venom of the spitting and the clanging of the hammer – all
these were in his mind as he spoke. 'He was reckoned among
the transgressors.' He was reckoned among the transgressors

by those who were themselves transgressors. 'Whomsoever I shall kiss, that same is he: hold him fast.' The soldiers closed in, there was no escape, it was the end, not the finish but the end in the sense that it was the beginning of all that would bring his work to its fruition. It was the beginning of the act which would transform his every other act by drawing all the acts of his earthly ministry into unity. 'The things concerning me have an end' – an end which he was set to accomplish. Our Lord here took one step towards the sublime, agonizing, terrible moment of life, the moment of powerful helplessness when his broken hands were fastened to the deformed tree. 'Whomsoever I shall kiss, that same is he: hold him fast.' But it was not the Lord who was held fast, it was Judas who was held, held in the power of the broken, mad images that whirled in the movements of his mind; from that moment his life was all nightmare.

There can be no making without breaking; what has been formed must be broken before it can be transformed. The breaking is painful, but all breaking and pain is lost sight of in the accomplishment of the transformation. The tree must be broken before the table or the plough can be made. The bread must be broken before acquaintanceship can be made into friendship. In giving there is the pain of labour, and the pain of parting with that which could be for your own comfort or safety or pleasure. To give often seems like tearing your possessions away from yourself and leaving yourself with nothing, whereas it is the attempt to acquire and keep what you acquire that sooner or later leaves you without anything at all. Judas, in his attempt to acquire money and security, broke trust, broke friendship, broke himself, broke the security he had in search of illusory safety. There is nothing safe but the risks of love – and love consists in breaking to make, and making only to give; in love of God and love of neighbour the breaking and the making and the giving are one.

The commandment is threefold: 'Thou shalt love the Lord thy God, thou shalt love thy neighbour as thyself'. Love god, love your neighbour, love yourself. Sin can be interpreted as the harm you do to yourself, and this is one of the clearest interpretations that the Gospel suggests. You are to be blamed for what you lose. What you try to keep you lose, what you give away enriches you, enabling you to give more. Judas in trying to keep his safety and importance, lost both. 'I have sinned in that I have betrayed the innocent blood.' 'And they said, What is that to us? See thou to that. And he cast down the pieces of silver.' Sin is the refusal to love yourself in other people; sin is the refusal to love yourself in God, sin is the refusal to love yourself wherever you find yourself. You are not confined within the bounds of your own being, there are no walls that shut in one life from the lives of others. We are distinct from one another, but not separate from one another. Our distinctness is such that we are responsible for all our deeds and for all our words. Our unity with one another is such that if I hate myself I hate all, and if I hate others I hate myself. Judas turned his love for our Lord into hatred, and ended by hating himself. The wish to destroy another contains within it a hidden threat to the safety of the destroyer. You cannot hate selectively; hatred of one ends up by being hatred of all, including the hater. You cannot love selectively either. In loving one you are loving all; you cannot love one if you do not love all. Whenever love is selective, it turns to hatred; whenever love strives to be all inclusive hatred dwindles. You cannot stop hating; you can only conquer your hating by the strength of your loving. The call of Christ is not a call to hate yourself and all men so that you may love him. The call of Christ may be stated in two ways: it is a call to love yourself and all men that you may love him; it is a call to love him so that you may love yourself and all men. 'Love one another the way I love you', he commands. He forms all that is, and transforms all he forms. He forms and transforms to give. He only forms to give; he only gives to form. We are to take what he has formed, and break it with the hands of our understanding and use it; whenever we use it truly, all men living can benefit. Bread can be used to form and deepen friendships; bread can be used to strengthen the strong, to comfort the weak and to deepen the rejoicing of the happy. Bread can be used as a threat or a bribe. Bread can be used to make those who possess it powerful. Men can destroy themselves in a longing to own more bread than they could ever need. We can use bread to pity, to patronize or to flatter – or worse, we can refuse to use it at all because we have ceased to love ourselves.

At the centre of our religion there are scraps of broken bread. A great deal of the understanding of our religion is given to us as we reflect on the scraps of broken bread. 'On the same night

that he was betrayed, he took bread and broke it.' The hands
that took the bread made the bread, and the hands that made
the bread broke the bread and gave the bread. To every man a
scrap of bread, a scrap from the same loaf – for all are made to
be one in him and he is the peace and sustenance of all. Sin is
fragmentation. Sin is the claim of the individual to be exclusive
in his love or selective in his hatred. The hands that broke the
bread, the hands that were broken and fastened to the Cross are
powerful enough, patient enough, to gather up the fragments
that remain after every human sin.

THE BREAKING OF BREAD (3)

MATTHEW 26 26-29; MARK 14 22-25; LUKE 22 19-20

'In the same night that he was betrayed he took bread and
when he had given thanks, he broke it and gave it to his
disciples.'

They had often heard him use the words of the
thanksgiving:

'Blessed be Thou, O Lord our God, eternal King,
Who bringest forth bread from the earth.'

They had often watched the movements of his hands as he
broke the bread and gave to each of them a scrap from the
broken loaf. They had often and often joined with him in that
prayer of thanksgiving which they knew so well; they had
often and often taken into their hands the scrap of the broken
loaf which he gave them. Every time they shared the broken
loaf with him was an expression of their union with him and
with one another in him. The broken loaf was an assurance of
their wholeness in him. Often and inevitably that wholeness in
him was broken both by the sins of each and by the common
sins of all. They were often absurdly pleased with themselves,
they sometimes thought that they deserved high rewards for
what they had given and for what they had done already; they
even argued about who should be greatest. Even on the same
night that he was betrayed they argued about who should be
the greatest. As the hour of the betrayal approached there must
have been something regal, something magnificent and
powerful in his bearing that they interpreted as the approach of
his victory. There is always something of that magnificence in
the bearing of a martyr. In our day, in our part of the world,
there are martyrs; there are those who answer the call of God
when the work he gives them can only be done through slow
martyrdom, not the quick martyrdom of execution, but the
slow martyrdom of bearing the deadening blows dealt by the
apathetic, the indifferent, the hostile and all those who consider
our religion a fairy tale and the King of glory a phantasy of the
deluded. The power the martyr wields is the power of
submission: 'He gave his cheek to the smiters'; but there can be

LOVE OF THE WORLD

no submission without confrontation; it is the manner of submission that makes the martyr, not the kind of death he dies. The martyr's life for the Lord in earth hastens his physical death, just as all work in earth hastens physical death. Even at the approach of his martyrdom they argued about which of them should be greatest – the oldest of all human arguments. He stripped himself of his outer garments and came to them dressed as a slave and carrying the basin and the towel to do the task of a slave. A menial service had been forgotten, and he was coming to them that what had been overlooked should be done. The disciples shrank from him and their shrinking is expressed in the words of Peter: 'Lord, dost thou wash my feet?' They who argued about who should be greatest were to see where true greatness resides. 'We are what we receive', says Augustine. Greatness resides in receiving, not primarily in giving. We have nothing that we have not received, what we give has already been given us. Service of the Lord begins, and can only begin, through accepting his service. He who receives little, gives little. Pride always finds receiving more difficult than giving, and therefore finds the ability to give small.

There are broken scraps of bread at the centre of our religion, and near the centre is a towel and basin, for it is only by accepting the most menial services of the Lord that we can also accept his treating us as if we were equals, which is the meaning of the broken loaf. In each case we are to accept what he offers. What have we to give him that he has not already given us? But that is to think of love as a nicely balanced matter of giving and receiving and receiving and giving. In the divine love the distinction between giving and receiving is blurred; the emphasis is rather on using and enjoying.

But let us look again at the figure in the garments of a slave carrying the towel and the basin; let us look at the signs of astonishment and dismay in the faces of the disciples. In looking we see that we can only be at peace with God by accepting the fact that he knows and always has known the very worst about us. He sees quite clearly the things about ourselves that we try to hide from our own gaze and blot out of our knowledge of ourselves. He knows things about us worse than the things we know about ourselves. We are to accept the fact that he knows. Human friendship consists in friends recognizing the shamefulness as well as the goodness of one

another and of their friendship. It tests your love of another to
bear the fact that he knows your disgraces as well as your
generosity. In life it is always strengthening and healing when
another knows your meannesses and cowardices and is
compassionate without being scornful or humiliating you in
any way. This compassion needs little more to express it than
an absence of shrinking and repugnance; this compassion is
not the result of an act of will in the moment of another's
sudden, or suddenly known, disaster; this compassion is the
fruit of a lifetime's love of truth; this compassion is the
resurrection of pride killed by love and rising again as humility.
What we destroy, God transforms; compassion is superiority
transformed. We destroy the evil in us by our clumsy deeds of
love for our neighbour – that love, despite confusion of mind
and uncertainty of feelings, is cleansed by the power of the
divine touch. These deeds may be no bigger than a gentleness
in the gaze, an absence of hauteur in the bearing; such things
are only small when measured quantitatively. These deeds
spring from the moments when we seem to be swept into
awareness that we hold and are held by a love which makes
men and things and God a unity. We only really live when we
cease to bother about the distinctions between giving and
receiving, between actions and results, between faithfulness
and rewards, between mine and thine, between ours and
theirs. We only really live when we know ourselves as persons
with an individual responsibility and as beings who are parts of
the whole creation of God. We are meaningless when we are
considered singly; we are meaningful when considered as
living centres of being within the totality of being. We know
ourselves, not by searching for ourselves but through the acts
of prayer by which we long to know as we are known and love
as we are loved. These longings in our prayers are also
expressed whenever we act as if the shame and glory of others
were our own. The words 'as if' are false; the shame and glory
of others are our own.

At the centre of our religion there are scraps of bread, there is
also a towel and a basin. The hands that took and broke the
bread were taken and broken and fastened to the Cross. He
who stripped himself of his outer garments and took the towel
and the basin was stripped by his enemies and was tortured,
derided and killed. We can only see the meaning of the broken

loaf when we look at the dark Cross on the hillside and there we also know something of the significance of the towel and the basin. It is only the glorious that can free us from the contamination of sordid acts; the glorious act is perfect might expressed in perfect mercy. Perfect mercy is represented for us both by the stripped figure at the disciples' feet and by the stripped figure on the Cross. But mercy is also represented for us by the shared loaf at the supper table. 'I have called you friends', he said. Our friendship with him is not the friendship of equals: he does not consider price and think of debt. Affection neither measures cost nor balances receiving with giving. Love does cost both lover and beloved, but the cost can only be paid when it is forgotten by both. Gratitude is not the sense of a debt to be paid, for giving is unconditional; gratitude lies in the use of the gift. 'This is my body which is given for you.' We always connect the broken loaf on the table with the broken body on the Cross. Let us take what is given, let our hands be steady and our minds certain. He who gives also helps us to receive. Neither cringing nor presumption will do instead of penitence; penitence cannot be forced, it comes to us as we look at our Lord and it is lost in his insistence that we forget inequalities and take what he gives.

THE AGONY IN THE GARDEN

'Likewise after supper he took the cup, and when he had given thanks he gave it to them saying, Drink ye all of this, for this is my blood of the new testament which is shed for you and for many . . .'

He, the maker of all that is, took the loaf and the cup into his hands and shared them with his disciples. Sometimes we think in a flash of apprehension that we understand all that he was doing; more often apprehension is dim but real, and real enough to know participation contains within it the only certain apprehension. To share the loaf and the cup is to find in adoration that which analysis could not uncover. In the moment of adoration, reason is to be stilled, but it must be neither destroyed nor silenced. Reason deepens adoration; adoration widens reason's gaze.

'Likewise after supper he took the cup.' The meal must end; one by one the men leave their places, the lamp is extinguished and the door is closed. He who took the cup at the supper table shrank from the cup in the garden. 'Father, all things are possible unto thee; take away this cup from me; nevertheless, not what I will, but what thou wilt.' 'Take this cup from me . . .' Nerves tighten and tremble, the whole body becomes taut and distraught in the anticipation of physical ordeal – the scourge is felt before it falls, the nails are sharpest before they are driven. Tight trembling nerves make difficult the mind's resistance to the doubts that traverse it and the anxiety that shakes it in the last moments before irrevocable action. The body's instability may be mastered, doubts and anxiety quietened in the mind, but there is a final struggle in which the position won may be worse than lost. That is the struggle against the temptation to give up the resolution because the good contemplated and determined would provide the occasion for the temptation of others. Is the good act sufficient reason to risk leading others into temptation through its performance?

'Take away this cup from me.' Must it be that these poor sleeping friends are to be overpowered by their fears so that they run blindly through the night to safety and to their own despair? Must it be that Peter in the dawn will cry like a child frightened by the light and the strange sounds of a new day? Must it be that Mary will be pierced by the sword she has made sharp for herself by her love? Must it be that witnesses will perjure themselves, that rulers will misuse their powers and Pilate betray humself? Must it be that when the time comes soldiers will contend for the discarded cloak while thoughtless people participate in a cruelty they do not understand?

The reverence for him that leads us to attempt to understand him must also prevent us from shaping conclusions about him that are unwarranted. Reverence should not be intrusive; it should not attempt to invade the mystery of the agony of the Lord. We are not to carry ourselves away with speculations about him and at the same time we are not to let fear of error paralyse our thoughts about him; we are not to stifle reflection so as to avoid the irreverence of presumption. What is begun in our love for him will be corrected on account of his love for us. Love has its peculiar risks. In love of God the risk of presumption is greater reverence than the refusal to reflect in the name of safety.

Whatever else is contained in the mystery of his agony in the dark garden, the prayer he used is for deliverance from temptation. We know that temptations never repeat themselves; there may be re-echoes of former voices and the re-grouping of former images, but the sound of the voices and the pattern of the re-grouping are always different. There is a familiarity and a freshness about all temptations; they come as they are expected, but not in a form that can be anticipated and they are always most powerful when we are making the best affirmations. The affirmations our Lord made on the mountain top were the occasion for the most acute temptations. 'If thou be the Son of God . . .' The affirmation in the garden is the occasion for the repetition of a familiar temptation and the familiar is always expressed in a new form. 'Father, all things are possible unto thee; take away this cup from me; nevertheless, not what I will, but what thou wilt.'

Conflict is the prelude to creation. As torch after torch illuminates the garden, as sword after sword comes gleaming out of the shadows, we see the trap closing – torch-bearers, sword-bearers, chief priests, Pilate, the crowd – all are caught in it, and he, the prisoner, is free. To give freedom he must be free, and he is free though his hands are bound and the judges are waiting.

THE VIA DOLOROSA

LUKE 23

'Daughters of Jerusalem, weep not for me, but weep for yourselves and for your children. For, behold the days are coming in which they shall begin to say to the mountains. Fall on us! and to the hills, Cover us! For if they do these things in a green tree, what shall be done in the dry?'

He, who came dressed as a slave, carrying the basin and the towel, now stumbles under the weight of the cross he carries. His brow is scarred with wounds made by the thorns; the hands that were with the hands of the disciples on the supper table now grasp the rough wood of the cross. Lately branches were strewn in his path and cheer followed cheer. There is no cheering now; there are shouts and there is cruel laughter. In a lull between the shouts and the laughter women can be heard weeping. His voice is clear: 'Daughters of Jerusalem, weep not for me, but weep for yourselves and for your children.'

We are not to weep for anyone who has found something greater to do with life than make the attempt to prolong it. We are certainly not to weep for him. The stumbling figure on the Via Dolorosa shows that stumbling is the only gait and the Via Dolorosa the only way. He shows that the only power is the power to bear pain in the furtherance of a purpose made clear by the demands of love. The Via Dolorosa is not the way of resignation but of determination, it is not to be thought of as self-abnegation but as self-affirmation. The Via Dolorosa does not mark the difference between love without power and power without love; the movement of the stumbling feet expresses the power of love. 'If my kingdom were of this world then would my servants fight.' He carries the cross and not the sword; he does not bear the cross in vain, for both cross and sword have power. 'Weep not for me . . .' Achievement is born out of conflict; struggle is the stuff of life. The moment of the crucifying is a moment of creation. The procession from the garden full of shadows and the procession to the place of the crucifying are not occasions for pity. We are not to confuse pity for him with repentance. Whenever we look at the stumbling figure our tears are to be for ourselves and for our fellows. Singly and collectively we so often refuse the Via Dolorosa; we refuse, and choose the sword rather than the cross; or else we hesitate in choice, the sword is too cruel and the cross too foolish. To choose the cross is to choose the pain and the glory of self-affirmation in the name of him in whom we live and move and have our being. This is losing your life for his sake to save it for his sake. Self-affirmation means awareness of the size of life, its contradictions, its bewildering demands on wisdom, patience, subtlety, imagination. Self-affirmation means recognizing the nature and the source of the doubts that cross and recross your mind; it makes you a prey to the anxiety that haunts you lest in affirming yourself you are in reality denying and destroying yourself. The higher your proper ambitions the fiercer and stronger will be your temptations – self-affirmation strengthens tensions that are powerful enough to tear you apart. Self-affirmation teaches much about being alone, about being misunderstood, applauded or attacked for the wrong reasons; it has some knowledge of love rejected, and of love of man being substituted for love of God. Self-affirmation is to know that realm of life where safety and danger change their usual meanings; it is to live in that realm surrounded by derision, mockery, pity, suspicion and dread – all of which are forgotten in the moments when the peace that passeth all understanding stills the understanding.

To look at the passion of our Lord is to see what the Lord of life is expressing through bread and wood and stone. It is to look at the broken bread on the table, the broken body on the Cross and the broken tomb in the garden. To look at the passion is to realize that you are seeing yourself; and that you are being called to partake of the bread on the table, the sufferings of the body on the Cross and the triumph shown by the stone. 'Weep not for me in my agony', says our Lord. 'Weep for yourself and look to your own.' On the Via Dolorosa he turned to the weeping women and there was rebuke in his voice. 'Weep not for me . . .' In the garden at the dawn there was no rebuke in his voice when he spoke. The surprise of peace can be unbearable and bewildering; it can look like illusion. Those who truly sorrow only look for peace in truth and truth in peace; love looks without greed and finds in wordless gratitude. 'Woman why weepest thou?' He does not rebuke her tears.

At the end of the Via Dolorosa is the place of crucifixion; the moment of crucifixion is a moment of creation, the agony and the joy are one in him, who is 'the author and finisher of our faith, who for the joy that was set before him endured the cross, despising the shame, and is set down at the right hand of the throne of God.'

THE EUCHARIST

'It would be easy to be a saint if you hadn't to bother about being human.' The authentic Christian reply would be that the only way to be human is to be a saint. Rub these two aphorisms together – the sparks that fly give a brief light and in their light it is possible to see much that otherwise might be hidden from the understanding.

Grace does not destroy nature: grace transforms nature. Grace is freely given, but it must be freely received. To receive grace, of course, is a manifold activity, and consequently the description is manifold. We never dare think about receiving grace or talk to others about receiving grace unless at the same time we are describing to ourselves and to others how it is possible to set about performing this manifold activity. To receive grace is to allow oneself to be aware of one's full human size. To allow oneself to be aware of one's full human size is not one simple act performed once and for all. It is the constant awareness of one's relationship with things and with persons who in turn are bound up in the complexity of group and inter-group relationships. It is the constant awareness that an individual is a living part of a living totality. This kind of awareness is a participation described by Eliot's analogy when he speaks of:

'Music heard so deeply that
it is not heard at all,
But you are the music while
the music lasts.'

We know the awareness that is participation when we are enthralled by the nightingale's clear, pure note or the savage crash of wave after wave on the dark unyielding rocks. We know what Donne means when he says: 'Every man's death diminishes me.' We know that the shame and glory of humanity is part of us: we know a strange peace when we see the lines and contours of the face of one who is old in years and in piety; we know a feeling far deeper than sentimental disturbance or righteous indignation when we note the figures that move in and out of the shadows of city streets. The burden of original sin bends us down and stunts our growth. Mankind made in the image of God is shattered into fragments by all who seek to control a separate destiny of their own design. We are all prey to the anger, lust, pride and envy which do not spring from our conscious will. Sin is the attempt to enlarge ourselves which is in practice a narrowing of ourselves; he that exalteth himself shall be abased. To receive grace is to struggle for size, the size that is ours as parts of the totality, but not as masters of the totality. The nature of the struggle and the goal of the struggle are clearly seen, but not in detail, when we contemplate the mysteries of both the unconsecrated bread and wine and the consecrated bread and wine.

MEDITATION ON THE EUCHARIST

(Our saviour Jesus Christ), who in the same night
that he was betrayed, took bread; and, when
he had given thanks, he brake it, and gave
it to his disciples, saying, Take, eat, this
is my Body which is given for you: Do this
in remembrance of me. Likewise after supper
he took the Cup; and, when he had given
thanks, he gave it to them, saying, Drink
ye all of this; for this is my Blood of
the New Testament, which is shed for you
and for many for the remission of sins:
Do this, as oft as ye shall drink it, in
remembrance of me.

Book of Common Prayer

To reflect on the Eucharist includes reflection on Maundy Thursday night; Maundy Thursday night – the night of the Betrayal, the Agony, the Desertion. The night of the Betrayal – Judas, the high priests, the clink of silver coins shining in the lamplight. The night of the Agony – the night of mysterious distress in the moonlit garden where the twisted branches of the olive trees threw shadows over the One who prayed. The night of the Desertion – eleven breathless men, their eyes wide with terror and shame, shame for their fear, and fear of their fear and the consequences of their desertion. Maundy Thursday night – the night of broken things, the many-imaged night where all images are dominated and understood by one image, the movement of hands taking the Bread and taking the Cup.

To reflect on that night is to lose the immediate sense of clocks and calendars and to gain a new awareness of the movements at the still point where time and timelessness are one; the movements at the still point are the movements of God in us and us in God. We cannot say of what happened on Maundy Thursday night that what happened happened long ago; acts are endless by their nature, and in this quality of endlessness what has been done in what we call the past is a living part of what we call the present. Acts are performed at a particular point in time but they are completed at infinity, for all acts begin in God and end in him; the evil act is a perverse use of what he makes and does, and runs its painful course through the lives of men; the good act is the good use of what God makes and gives and it also runs its course through the lives of men till it comes to its fruition in him in whom it had its origin. I am Alpha and Omega, saith the Lord, the beginning and the end. In the Eucharist we remember the past, the present, the future. We remember what God has done, what God is doing and what God will do; we give thanks for the Birth, Life, Death, Resurrection, Ascension of the Lord whereby we are delivered from the bondage of sin and death and time, and given again the glorious liberty of the Children of God. To use the word 'remember' in connection with the Eucharist has a certain necessity and certain difficulties. The Eucharist is not a memorial service; to do the Eucharist is to participate in a victory, the victory of God. The spirit of the Eucharist is not explained by comparing it with the spirit of Ash Wednesday or of Good Friday. The hands that broke bread on Maundy Thursday night were fastened, helpless, to the Cross, but it was those same hands which burst open the helpless Tomb. Our response to the Eucharist is continually being enlarged by the vastness of the Eucharist.

The Eucharist cannot be explained; to use exact language in thinking about it is to be gravely inaccurate. To consider the Eucharist leads us to describe and to adore. Before the altar we may be aware of consolation or desolation; we may know the plenitude of peace or the emptiness that pains. Whatever such immediate awareness may be there is a deeper happening, a growth of certainty and confidence, of joy and peace, of power and purpose, of hope and its fulfilment. This profound happening may be only dimly perceived; it seldom manifests itself in forms that are easily discernible, except perhaps by others. To take part in the Eucharist is to find oneself drawn out into an immensity that cannot be contained in time or space. In the Eucharist we are blessed with consciousness, which is usually more clear than comfortable, but the pain of truth is part of every joy. In the Eucharist we are blessed with consciousness: 'To be conscious is to be out of time.' We do not attain consciousness either by neglect of the things of this transitory world or by pushing between them out into the wider world. There are no gaps between the things of this transitory world; they form together a living pattern. We go through the things of this transitory world to the beyond; we do not leave them behind, we bring them with us; they are transformed with us at the touch of God, who is for ever drawing us into consciousness, away from the existence that is in day-dreams, away from fitful glances at reality and concern for trivialities that is no more than nervous occupation.

We go through the things of time to the beyond, we bring the things of time with us, we cannot disentangle ourselves from them. We do not move in space or place to arrive in the beyond . . . the beyond is within us. This is implied, perhaps, in that through common bread and wine, things of time, we are drawn into the mystery of the intimacy of God, in whom we live and move and have our being.

In the Eucharist we are constantly bringing our attention back to God's creatures of Bread and Wine. Before consecration and after consecration they are doors that open, they are glimpses of the immensity and you are what you see as the vision lasts: this is a way of saying that in the Eucharist we are a living part in the whole created order in time and out of time. 'This is my Body which is given for you . . .', says the Lord of life, without whom nothing was made that was made, in whom all things cohere.

We do not look at the mysteries of our faith, we cannot explore them and carry back report. We are part of the mysteries ourselves; we have only to turn our eyes inward to realise our manifold connection with things and people in God in whom we know ourselves, in whom we live and move and have our being. In the Eucharist we realise our participation in the mysteries of creation and redemption. Creation is not completed, we have our active part in its continuous work. 'He who made us without our aid, will not save us without our co-operation.' A gift to be used rather than a thing done for us is the analogy for redemption. 'He took Bread . . . and brake it and gave it to them . . .' His hands broke the bread, their hands were extended to receive it. The hands that broke the bread made the bread. No bread is made without him. He declares that 'Man doth not live by bread alone.' He also shows that man in this world cannot live without bread. He is the maker both of bread and the things other than bread by which human life is possible. On Maundy Thursday night the common bread became the uncommon bread to satisfy the common needs. Before reflecting on the consecrated bread and wine, there must always be reflection on the unconsecrated bread and wine, for the mystery of redemption only becomes fully meaningful through consideration of the mystery of creation.

God brought life into being without our aid, he does not sustain it without our effort. The unbroken loaf on the altar is an expression of the endless love of God. It reminds us that friendship, imagination, ingenuity, intelligence, determination, memory are just as much parts of creation as the baked loaf. The divine generosity provides us with endless raw materials which we use to bring into being the richness of melody, the nuances of poetry, the sensitiveness of drama, the inventors' daring and the electricians' deftness, the bakers' skill and the lorry drivers' nerve. The unbroken loaf on the altar can start a whole procession of images in our minds: the brown broken earth, the rhythm of the sower's movements; the cornfield, a golden sea slowly swaying and sighing in the autumn breeze. We see the gyrations of vast engines, the white-clothed figures in the bakery and fleets of coloured motor vans. The rotation and hum of the machinery is as much a part of creation as the slow swaying and sighing of the cornfield in the autumn breeze.

The scientist breaks bread and reports to us that bread can ultimately be broken into space and energy, continuous movement marvellously confined in a particular shape. Many have been drawn into a fuller consciousness through investigation of the unconsecrated bread, they pause to wonder and incoherently praise the unnamed and unnameable power that ceaselessly fashions and re-fashions in a manner largely inscrutable. 'Ye worship ye know not what,' said St. Paul in respect and in compassion. The scientist breaks bread and reports a mystery; the modern physicist holds that a simple explanation in terms of cause and effect does not explain the sequences of happenings in the physical world. The priest breaks bread and reports a mystery: 'The Body of our Lord Jesus Christ which was given for you . . .' And here no simple explanation in terms of cause and effect will explain the sequence of happenings. The broken bread, the broken body, the broken tomb, the oneness of all creatures in him in whom all fullness dwells cannot be connected together in our understanding by a simple rational process. We do not attempt to explain where we can only make descriptions, we do not continue to analyse where we can only wonder and adore. Within the Eucharist is the endlessness of the divine energy and the spaciousness in which every generation is included with room enough left for those yet to be. This energy and this space is contained in a shape whose outline is too distant for us to see; within this shape the pattern of every Eucharist is woven with strands made from the things of time and with strands made from the timeless things. Each altar is an everywhere, and the time is always now. The worshippers meet at a moment in time, but the Eucharist is: 'A moment in and out of time.' Only through time is time conquered. We do not push between the things of this transitory world out into the wider world. The bread is broken, the wine is poured out, the creatures of time become the means by which we transcend time: we today are as close to the Lord of life and death as the disciples were on Maundy Thursday night; there we are with angels and archangels and all the company of heaven, for Eucharist is: 'At the still point of the turning world.' The still point is where this world and the other world interpenetrate. At the still point, clock and calendar, maps drawn to scale and speed in travel are all transcended. Through the mystery of the blessing and the breaking and the taking of bread and wine we find:

> '. . . the impossible union
> Of spheres of existence is actual,
> Here the past and the future
> Are conquered and reconciled.'

Here is the place, here is the moment when what we do with
the unconsecrated bread can be reconciled with what we do
with the consecrated bread. Here it is that the business of hands
with the things of time is seen as not necessarily inconsistent
with those same hands being extended to receive the things
that are not of time. Here it is seen that the conversation round
the fire need not necessarily be out of keeping with the chorus
of praise in the Sanctus. In this earth we have our place in the
great company of the redeemed. We are people who live in the
past and in the future, for past, present, future are one in God.
We are in time and out of time:

> '. . . But to apprehend
> The point of intersection of the timeless
> With time, is an occupation for the saint –
> No occupation either, but something given
> And taken, in a lifetime's death in love,
> Ardour and selflessness and self-surrender.'*

In the Eucharist we are given what we neither deserve nor
understand: we give more than we understand, for we give
what God has first given us, we have nothing else to give. The
moment of the Eucharist is a moment lived in time and also
lived beyond the horizons of both time and space where, with
angels and archangels and all the company of heaven we know
the praise we cannot utter.

* T. S. Eliot, Four Quartets – The Dry Salvages.

THE EUCHARIST AND THE COMMON LIFE
IN THE CHURCH

At present many are concerned about freedom, knowledge and group life. Men and women guard their freedom but at the same time are reluctant to make choices.

People are disturbed by the increasing human knowledge and a growing sense of the fragmentary nature of all human knowledge. The limitations of human knowledge are clearly seen in the realisation that a group can never entirely be under the control of its members either severally or all together.

A study of the Eucharist, as well as participation in it, may help us to be free, to appreciate the knowledge we have and to be more sensitive in accepting the responsibilities through the groups to which we belong. At the same time a study of freedom, knowledge and group life may enrich our participation in the eucharistic act. A single meditation with this width of subject can do no more than make suggestion, indeed such a subject cannot be brought to a rounded-off conclusion and so is best thought of as a series of reflections on freedom, knowledge and group life remembering that Christian doctrine shows us not what to think about such subjects but how to think about them.

The eucharistic act is complex and capable of many descriptions. Here, for the time, it is described as the celebration of the greatness of God who became man without ceasing to be God that men might be godly without ceasing to be men. This action is the birth, life, death, resurrection and ascension of our Lord by which we are set free from the fear of sin and time and death and the narrowness of this present world. This action has no simple automatic effect on men and women: it calls for a response, and the response can only be made by the whole activity of a man's life broken up and interrupted by sins and repentance. To put it in another way, the Eucharist is the celebration of the goodness of God who gives all things, visible and invisible, to us on one condition, that we receive them. This receiving is the activity of a lifetime and consists in using the gifts broken up and interrupted by sins and repentance as this using may be. At the height of the eucharistic celebration the experience of giving and receiving is replaced by a sense of the joy of being alive in a world God loves and in the church he has called into being. What has been said in this paragraph could well be supplemented and expanded by meditation on these words of our Lord and of St. Paul: 'Freely ye have received; freely give;' (Matthew 10 8); 'All things are yours' (I Corinthains 3 21), especially the things given us in the celebration of the Eucharist.

Every fully human act is free but not fully free because only perfect love can cast out fear and where there is fear there cannot be complete freedom. The celebration of the Eucharist is a human act though not fully free. It is more than distasteful to think of people being forced, directly or indirectly, to participate in the celebration. Worship begins in the free choice of the worshipper to respond to the calling of God through and above all people and things. This act is made possible by the free act of accepting, first, the fragmentary nature of all human knowledge; secondly, that men and women are conditioned by tradition and environment. A man loses his freedom if he hesitates to act until he knows the meaning and results of whatever acts he may have a mind to perform. Thus the communicant must give himself over to the movement of the Eucharist without trying to find out what is happening to him and to his fellow communicants. He knows that there are moments of perfect love in it which one should not desire but hope to recognise. Knowledge is never to be set aside on the grounds that faith is sufficient. Faith makes knowledge possible: here, faith in the meaningfulness of the Eucharist enables us to celebrate it and to grow in understanding of it, but first communicants must be free from the fear of being caught up in the mystery of the creative activity of God. To be free means acceptance of the limitations of all human knowledge and to accept the fact that we are conditioned by tradition and environment. For good or bad, twentieth century people can think and wish in a manner impossible for any other generation. The reasons are many: for instance speedy communication and transport, the increase in population, the rapid building of new cities and towns, the restlessness of life inevitable for all who merely wish to be free and find life difficult insofar as the former regional groups are broken up. Environment and tradition cannot be considered separately for a great deal of environment is made up by the conflict between those who reject and those who accept the traditional modes of behaviour. The Christian appreciates both tradition and environment without being blinded by either, and knowing that his individuality (and sanctity) depends on his bearing the tension between himself and both tradition and environment.

Christianity, while never losing sight of the importance of the individual, is essentially the common life of a group of people. This fact is often blurred in the minds of people who know the weaknesses of local church groups in their week-to-week living compared with the doctrine of the church as called into being by God and sanctified by him to love the world as he loves it. Neither the individual nor the Christian group achieves sinlessness in this world no matter how devout individuals and groups may be. Individuals are tempted and fall into sin; the life of the group can be aimless, banal or merely amiable or fussy to no discernible purpose. Whenever this happens Christian individuals and groups distort the gospel, yet the Christian way of life cannot be without the common activities of the group and the personal holiness of its members. In most localities the serious heresies are manifested by the Christian group's activities, particularly by those other than the common worship of the group. The fact that the life of the church groups is often so weak, flabby or museum-like leads to the fact that many are prepared to accept and expound Christianity as a philosophy of life but not as the common life of a group. Even theologians, unknowingly, deny the fundamental corporate nature of Christianity. Churchmen can sympathise with this tendency if they know how difficult any group life is and how specially difficult a church group can be. How often do church members make the affirmation 'I believe in the Holy Catholic Church' with very mixed feelings? This is because they cannot forget responsibility for both their individual sins and for the corporate sins of the group. Group acts are more often dictated by weakness rather than by misplaced zeal. Reflection on the behaviour of the disciples throughout the first Maundy Thursday night does much towards an understanding of the church in terms of group life. The church has its tremendous moments when it celebrates the glory of God in the Eucharist but members will be concerned for their own greatness, they will run away from glory, they will deny the glory and they will return to it or try to forget what they have done or left undone.

When St. Paul talks of the group life of the church he insists
that all members have not the same office (see Romans 12 and
First Corinthians 12). He reminds his readers that the church is
like the human body because each member has its distinct
function in every bodily activity, giving a dynamic picture of
the church as a diversity in unity. At present many churchmen,
implicitly and frequently, give the impression that all members
have the same function, namely, evangelisation. Consequently
clergy and laity are trained to be evangelists, to be intellectuals,
to the incoherent and the inarticulate as well as to a section of
society which some hold does not exist. Some church members
underline the lack of leaders and prophets and make
suggestions about training members for leadership and
leaving priests free from administration to develop their
prophetic powers. But laymen can be prophets and those who
can recognise prophets are nearly as scarce as prophets ('he
that receiveth a prophet in the name of a prophet shall receive a
prophet's reward,' Matthew 10 41). The life of the body depends
on the high use of gifts and talents of its several members. The
body wanes when the gifted and talented are few and this
scarcity is a judgement on the group life of the church here in
earth.

Group life exists through the common actions of its
members; these actions must be exciting and meaningful
though their meaning is never completely understood. This
can only be when the group hold common faith and share a
common purpose. The celebration of the Eucharist is the most
important activity of Christian groups, every communicant is
not a liturgiologist or a person of deep spiritual perception.
Many communicants would not talk intelligently about the
meaning of what is done in the Eucharist as illuminated by the
whole body of Christian doctrine. This inability in itself does
not indicate defective group life because theologians
(academic, liturgiologists, pastors etc.), are called to watch all
the activities of the group, eucharistic and otherwise. Like all
men, theologians are corruptible and offer false simplifications
or judge words and deeds pragmatically rather than
doctrinally. People of deep spiritual perception (clerics and
laity) help the group to know that the broken bread is the true
and living bread. All members have a special responsibility to
preserve the Eucharist from being falsified by the caprice of

priests and people in their group. Caprice is responsible for
defects in the group's non-eucharistic activities. Our Lord's
mandate was: 'love one another as I have loved you; by this
shall all men know that ye are my disciples.' (St. John 13 34-35)
St. John reminds us that this mandate was given on the same
night that the disciples argued about which of them should be
the most important and that they all of them fled at the first sign
of danger . . . and that after the breaking of bread and the
blessing of the cup and their declaration of unswerving loyalty
to him come prison, come death. In contemporary groups
some want office without toil and the painfulness of
responsibility, others want all the important work and the pain
involved. Clergy want laity to undertake impossible tasks; laity
feel that clergy are not as diligent in doing the possible as they
might be.

Dissension in a church group blurs spiritual discernment,
denies men their proper spiritual nourishment: a group can
deteriorate as an individual may in one of many ways –
complacency, insipidity, apathy, boredom, apostasy. The
church holds that the efficacy of the Sacrament does not
depend on the worthiness of the minister. Can the same be said
of the group? Or is it indeed possible that priest and people,
unknowingly, can join in an act which is not the Christian
Eucharist?

THE EUCHARIST AND THE LIFE OF MANKIND

If God does not exist everything is nightmare. If God does not exist there is no order, no sense, no knowledge, no coherency. Belief in God is belief in order, sense, knowledge and coherency.

In the beginning God created the heavens and the earth.
The earth was without form and void,
And darkness was upon the face of the deep;
And the Spirit of God was moving over the face of the waters.
And God said, 'Let there be light';
And there was light.

GENESIS 1 1-3

With the poet we look at the dark emptiness that was before the beginning; a dark emptiness in which there was no sound, no light, no movement. With none but the eyes of God to see and none but the ears of God to hear, the dark waters moved and the first sounds were heard. 'And the spirit of God moved upon the face of the waters, and God said, Let there be light' and so the whiteness of the first dawn was mirrored in the dark face of the waters.

In the beginning, God broke the stillness with movement;
In the beginning, God broke the silence with sound;
In the beginning, God broke the darkness with light.

Every act of creation is also an act of revelation; but if God only disclosed himself by means of sunset and storm, by thunder and tornado, by the green density of tropical forests and the bareness of distant mountain tops; if God only disclosed himself through the alterations from seed time to harvest and harvest to seed time; if God only disclosed himself through the brevity of temporal events, we would be lost in confusion. But:

In the beginning was the Word
And the Word was with God
And the Word was God.
He was in the beginning with God;

All things were made through him,
And without him was not anything made that
was made.
In him was life,
And the life was the light of men . . .
He was in the world,
And the world was made through him,
Yet the world knew him not.
He came to his own home,
And his own people received him not.
But to all who received him,
Who believed in his name,
he gave power to become children of God.

JOHN 1 1-4, 10-12

'He was in the world and the world was made through him . . .
He came to his own home and his own people received him
not.' 'The same night that he was betrayed, he took bread.' The
hands that took the bread made the bread. Every Eucharist sets
before us the mystery of creation as well as the mystery of our
redemption from the bondage of sin and death and time and
the whole world order.

'On the same night that he was betrayed, he took bread . . .'
He who took the bread made the bread he took. The
unconsecrated bread upon the altar focuses our attention on the
mystery of creation. The unconsecrated bread reminds us of the
golden sea of wheat rustling gently in the autumn breeze, the
drifting white clouds, the contours of the hills, the winding
dusty lanes, the weathered farm buildings serene in the
sunlight. God, who gives us bread, knowing that man cannot
live by bread alone, gives us beauty as well. The golden sea of
wheat rustles gently in the autumn breeze; the vast and
complicated machinery by which wheat becomes flour and by
which flour becomes bread moves rapidly and rhythmically,
humming and rattling. The sound of the breeze in the wheat
and the sound of machinery in movement are both parts of the
creation. Coal provides power to move the machinery into its
huge purposeful actions. Coal and this power are as much
parts of creation as the seed growing secretly and its green
shoots forcing their way through the earth. The seed could not
grow without sun and rain. Sun and rain are channels of the

life-giving energy of God. Sun and rain clouds are part of the
ordered movements of the whole universe; the growth of
wheat in one small field is dependent on series upon series of
movements within the whole planetary system. The farmer
who sows seed makes a change in the whole physical universe;
for the physical act of sowing sets in motion train after train of
physical events which will go on and on producing results until
the physical universe is brought to its conclusion in him in
Whom it had its beginning.

Bread could be called the transformation of rain and
sunshine. Bread could be called the storehouse of energy. The
scientist regards the smallest scrap of bread with wonder, none
of his formulae or all of them put together will exhaust the
physical marvels of bread. A piece of bread is a bit of matter,
and matter is the name for movement and space mysteriously
confined within a definite shape.

A particular piece of bread cannot be adequately described
without an attempt to describe the whole universe. Anything
we say about the universe must lead us to talk and think about
particular things, like pieces of bread. The unconsecrated bread
on the altar can be the starting point of our thinking about all
that is; if it is the starting point, all our thinking will bring us
back to it again.

The bread that we eat is transformed by eating into bodily
energy, the bread becomes a part of us; this process, like the
farmer sowing, is possible on account of numberless universal
movements. Every time we eat bread we remember that our
very physical existence depends upon the ceaseless work of
God. By his ceaseless work he constantly brings into being the
energy, physical and psychic, which we transform for our use;
he gives us all things to use, not to possess but to use. In the
beginning he forms all things; in his love he gives us the
power to transform what he has already formed; that is, he
makes us participants and not parasites. To use a phrase of St.
Athanasius, 'All our operations are co-operations' with him
who is the source of our life and light and power. It is love to
make to give; it is greater love to give so that others may be
makers. There is the lavish patronage which makes people into
paupers and dependents; there is the restrained giving of love
which enlarges the recipients. There is the gift that is far too
big, the gift that leaves the recipient nothing to do; there is the

gift which is just big enough to enable the recipient to act to the
height of his ability. Every gift of God's initiates and increases
human activity. The splendour of the sun initiates the
complexity of human labour which is clear before our minds
whenever we use bread as a focal point for reflection on the
mystery of creation.

> God said 'let us make man in our image,
> after our likeness; and let them have
> dominion over the fish of the sea,
> and over the birds of the air, and
> over the cattle, and over all the
> earth'.
>
> GENESIS 1 ²⁶

All things are ours, not by possessing them but by using them
according to our ability, by rejoicing in them according to our
love, and transforming them in accordance with the will of him
who 'has given the earth for the use of men.'

No one man can understand and rejoice in all things through
his own work alone. We rejoice and share in the work of others.
The precision of the scientist's work is as necessary to us as the
delicate and awe-inspiring sensibility and sensitivity of the
artist. The psychologist's knowledge is as necessary to us as
the fruits of the philosopher's discipline and the geologist's
discoveries. We are not to accept knowledge uncritically, but
we are to be critics, not sceptics. We are not to be disdainful
where we do not understand; we are to be discerning,
remembering that all knowledge begins in God, remembering
that the scientist's work and the theologian's work are both
necessary to us if our worship of God and our service of God
are to be mature. The scientist's formula, the theologian's
lucidity and restraint, the unconsecrated bread on the altar are
all parts of creation; none of them could be if God did not give
them being and sustain this being. The scientific formula is not
incapable of consecration, therefore we reverence it as we
reverence any scrap of unconsecrated bread wherever that
scrap may be and no matter who may have it. There is a proper
reverence for the consecrated bread; there is also a proper
reverence for the unconsecrated bread. The unconsecrated
bread on the altar reminds us of the reverence we are to show to

all created things. We remember that discoveries about created things are themselves also created things made through him without whom nothing is made that is made. Part of our reverence for all created things is our readiness to take seriously what serious people show to us about created things, whether these serious people are Christian people or not. Like the scribe, there are artists, scientists and social workers who are not far from the Kingdom; their fingers are often stretched towards the hem of the King's garment, sometimes they touch it and virtue goes out of him in whom all human work begins.

The unconsecrated bread on the altar reminds us of the vast complicated human activity there must be before bread can be made. Hundreds of thousands of people must live and work together before it is possible for us to eat a slice of bread, or to take bread and bless bread and break it as the Lord has bidden us. Every Eucharist is made possible, directly and indirectly, by hundreds and thousands of people, thousands of whom are non-Christian or consciously or unconsciously anti-Christian.

The policeman, the cabinet minister, the city electricians and plumbers and builders and countless more, by honest performance of their particular work make our Eucharists possible. We sometimes forget this except at vivid moments. In the roar and darkness and thunder of the skies in the Battle of Britain fighter pilots made it possible for the Eucharist to be celebrated at different places in this country. A large percentage of these pilots had never even seen the bread broken and the wine poured out. Of course there were exceptions and notable exceptions. But it always has been so, from Maundy Thursday onwards, that the celebration of the Eucharist is made possible by the co-operation of people who are never participants, who neither understand it nor care about it. In the Eucharist we use the work of architects, poets, musicians, many of whom know and show that art and bread alike are made by God who forms what we transform and even forms our power to transform. We also use the work of architects, poets and musicians who may be confused about God, who deny him and decry him. The life and aspirations of the godly and the ungodly, their doubts, their fears, their loves are all brought together in the mystery of the Eucharistic action. At neither font nor altar do we proclaim our disconnectedness with the whole human race; we renounce,

but we do not reject. The disciple cannot be different from his
Master; our Master came not to condemn, but to save. The
saving act contains within it no condoning of human sin. The
saving act is an act of compassion; in compassion there is
neither contempt nor condescension. The baptismal washing is
not after the type of Pilate's proclamation of his innocence of the
crime to which he acquiesced. At the altar we remember the
figure of the Lord, dressed like a slave, carrying the basin and
the towel to perform a menial service which had been left
undone. At the altar we can never be aloof, isolated, self-
contained. At the altar there is always a sense of contamination
as well as a realisation of sanctity; when we are at the altar we
are aware of our association with sinners and our fellowship
with angels and archangels and all the company of heaven.

There is always an awareness in the Eucharist of present
realities: the kind of realities represented by Judas, Pilate, the
Sadducees; the crowd roaring 'crucify!' and clamouring for
Barabbas; the disciples running blindly away from the Garden.
There are also the kind of realities typified by the good man of
the house and the man bearing the pitcher, by the woman
weeping in the Garden before the empty tomb. Just as the
unbroken bread on the altar is part of the whole physical
universe, so each individual present is part of the whole
universe of man that stretches out to include all who now have
their being in the realm of life that is beyond the horizons of
time and space. At the Eucharist in the breaking of bread the
gates of time are broken. Through things temporal we lay hold
on things eternal: all things are ours. The Eucharist is a
moment in and out of time, a brief moment of full
consciousness: to be conscious is to be out of time. 'And God
said 'Let us make man in our image, after our likeness; and let
them have dominion . . . over all the earth' '. If there were
perfect unity then the human dominion would be complete. Sin
limits and distorts this unity; sin thus limits human dominion.
The bread placed on the altar is the expression of the common
human destiny, to be one in God who is all in all. It is also a
visible expression of the present actuality, that is, the human
unity continually broken by sin after sin, yet in spite of
sinfulness we are able to live and praise God on account of
sufficient human co-operation. Though as I say these words,
we will all remember instances not too remote or too isolated

such as Bishop Wilson, later of Birmingham, illegally celebrating the Eucharist in a Japanese prison camp using half his day's rice ration and half his day's water ration. We are never far from the state of affairs where people in the following of their occupations, deliberately or indeliberately, make it difficult or impossible to celebrate the Eucharist. The Eucharist, sometimes by the very conditions in which it is celebrated and always by its very nature, reminds us of the brevity of all temporal security. The Eucharist also reminds us that the eternal security is neither brittle nor brief, though it sometimes appears to be too frail for testing and duration. On Maundy Thursday night our Lord was surrounded by the disciples stretching out their hands towards him . . . a few hours later the circle of swords and torches closed around him.

By birth we participate in the life of the whole human family in its universal setting. We share the glory of human achievements; we share human joys and sorrows and disappointments. We share the human grief and the human shame. By birth and life we know the mystery of iniquity and the mystery of goodness. We know these mysteries, not by sight but by the frequent warfare within us. We know what it is to 'wrestle not against flesh and blood, but against principalities, against powers, against the rulers of the darkness of this world, against spiritual wickedness in high places.' Unbaptised man knows the struggle, though he does not know it as acutely as we can nor would he describe it as we describe it. Every Eucharist reminds us that we are inextricably connected with the whole human race; at every Eucharist we see again that baptism does not divide us from the unbaptised but deepens our union with them by the responsibility given us for all men in our baptism. The way to discharge this responsibility is not easily seen, and is only seen in him who is the Beginning and the End, who maintains us and sustains us; even his chastisement is our peace, and his silence more clear than any speech.

THE EUCHARIST AND THE UNIVERSE

Neither death, nor life, nor angels,
nor principalities, nor things present,
nor things to come, nor powers, nor
height, nor depth, nor anything else
in all creation will be able to
separate us from the love of God in
Christ Jesus our Lord.

ROMANS 8 38-39

Every act of creation is an act of revelation. To reveal is not the mere presentation of a spectacle. To accept what is revealed is no mechanical or chance happening with fleeting consequences cancelled out by subsequent experiences. To see what is revealed means that your gait of thought is changed and the pattern of your feelings altered, the whole of life is re-orientated.

We cannot think about an object any way we like. The form of our thinking is dictated to us by the nature of the object we regard. Man is meant to extend the kind of control he exercises over his body so that this kind of control embraces more and more of the whole physical world of which man is a part. In studying an object a union is established in which an exact division between student and object is seen to be impossible. To turn St. Paul's words positively: death, life, angels, principalities, things present, things to come, height, depth, and all other creatures can lead us into the love of God which is in Christ Jesus our Lord.

Love always must have active expression. Love of God is actively expressed through love of his things: in our loving his things he draws us into union with him. To love his things is not to be confused with haphazard attention to what immediately attracts us. To love his things is an enduring, imaginative, intelligent and humble attention, which, of course, includes use of his things according to their nature. There is a way of regarding the cornfield that sways and sighs in the autumn breeze. There is a way of regarding the unconsecrated bread and wine upon the altar. There is also a way of regarding the consecrated bread and wine upon the altar which leads us into an awareness of the great mysteries of birth and life and death, of redemption and time and sin. There in the scrap of broken bread is dimly seen the triumph over death and life and principalities and powers, things present and things to come. It is a triumph that is not equivalent to total destruction. He did not come down from Heaven to unmake but to remake, to restore what sin has broken so that we are gathered up as fragments into the unity of men and angels where time and eternity, earth and Heaven lose their distinction in him who is our beginning and our end.

> Our Saviour Jesus Christ . . . in the same night that
> he was betrayed, took bread, and when he had
> given thanks, he brake it and gave it to his
> disciples . . . Likewise after supper, he took
> the cup, and when he had given thanks he
> gave it to them . . .
>
> Book of Common Prayer

To reflect on the Eucharist is to reflect on the mysteries of God and man, of creation and redemption; it is to reflect on our life in time and space and on our deliverance from the bondage of time and space by the same power which frees us from the prison of sin and death.

To reflect on the Eucharist is to see again the hands that moved in the lamplight. It is to sense again the stillness of the lamplit room, the stillness that was not merely absence of sound and movement. His voice broke the silence. He took the loaf into his hands; at that moment for the disciples there was nothing to be heard but the sound of his voice, nothing to be seen but the movement of his hands as he broke the flat Jewish loaf. The movement of his hands in the lamplight became for them, as for us, a lasting image which the whole pageantry of the mind's imagery does not obscure. It is the image in which countless images have their origin and their interpretation.

He took bread and broke it. Physically speaking, he performed an act of cosmic importance. Physicists tell us that every physical act sets in motion a complexity of happenings which go on reverberating long after the initial act has been performed. Every movement affects the whole pattern of energy within the universe. He took bread and broke it; physically speaking, he performed an act of cosmic importance, he performed an act which physically speaking had the timelessness characteristic of all acts. Physically speaking, an act is only to be described by postulating a complexity of causes and a complexity of results. Physicists are tentative in putting down either the causes or results, for the causes of a great many physical happenings are either obscure or apparently non-existent. The breaking of bread, at any time, by any person, physically speaking is more than we understand.

What of the agent who uses and sets in motion physical forces outside his knowledge or control? To speak of the agent in physical terms is to deal with the fact that no neat boundary between a man and the universe can fairly be made. You need air to breathe, you need the light to see by and to be seen, you need water to drink, food to eat and the earth to walk on. A man's body is his medium of expression, his means of communication. A man's body is so joined to the universe that he needs the whole universe to express himself and to be himself. A man is immanent in every expression of himself and at the same time there is a part of himself which he knows he can never express to any fellow-creature. His expressions of himself are so characteristic of him and yet so inadequate, so fragmentary. To express ourselves, to communicate with our fellows, we need the whole universe, we use the universe as if it were an extension of our body. At this present moment we owe our very being to physical happenings whose date is antique, whose force is operative now. To break bread at your own table with your friends is to perform physical acts of deep mystery and of far reaching consequences. The whole dynamic pattern of the universe's energy is affected, the effects will reverberate so long as the life of the universe continues. There is a timelessness about all acts which bewilders us till we overcome our rigid distinction between past, present and future. We are redeemed from time, from living on the edge of a double dread: the fear of what has been done and the fear of what is to come while we are enclosed in the prison of the present, regretting and waiting anxiously. To be redeemed is to be saved from both the past and the future and brought into the eternal present, for all time is one in God. In him, here and now, we are made strong to bear the burden of finiteness; in our faith we are reconciled to the puzzling knowledge given us by physicists; more than that, we know that to rejoice in such knowledge is to touch the hem of his garment.

To touch the hem of his garment is never enough and can never be as satisfying as to sit at his table, his known and invited guests. No matter how ill at ease we may be there, we know that it is where we should be rather than anonymously and timidly plucking the hem of his garment. It is right that he should be known in the laboratory, it is right that we should share, as far as we can, the exultation of physicists in the increase of our common human knowledge. We rejoice in the mysteries of the unconsecrated bread; at the Eucharist we specially rejoice in that it reminds us that the moments of time do not separate us from the deeds of God. We are as near to him who broke the bread on Maundy Thursday night as were Peter and James and John, and Thomas who had such difficulties. All are one in God, all times are one time in God.

'Nature has no outline, but imagination has.' Physically, we tend to divide the indivisible, we tend to isolate the units of creation and treat as separate what God made in unity. We tend to isolate the human body from the rest of matter, and, to use contemporary language, we tend to treat the human body as an autonomous centre of energy whereas it is a centre within a universal system. 'Nature has no outline, but imagination has.' When we use outlines we must be careful to describe a totality embracing each singular.

Psychically speaking, we tend to isolate the individual and treat him as a separate entity who breaches a gulf between himself and his fellows by an act of will or an act of love; the breaching is described in different ways. Psychically speaking we are, to use a metaphor, busy hotels rather than quiet detached villas. All sorts of people throng our premises and there is no closing time; even in sleep the doors are open for all who come and go. In spite of our togetherness each one of us is a unique individual who does not develop his uniqueness in isolation but in community. The mystery is mutely described in the Eucharist by the fact that one loaf is used but a piece is broken off from it for each individual. Man is made in the image of God; not individual man, but mankind – that is, mankind is a diversity in unity and a unity in diversity. Each man is public, inclusive, yet different from his fellows, unique. The claim of the individual to be selective, exclusive, private, aloof, is one way of talking about the sin that is the root of all sins – the sin of attempting to be a god, controlling one's own destiny; but no man could control his own destiny unless he also controlled the whole physical universe and whole world of men. The petition that asks 'Make an exception in my case, or in our case' needs to be carefully examined, just as the attitude that God will always take care of the universal at the expense of the individual proclaims the inability of God to be God, for God's care of the individual and the universal arouses no question of conflicting interests in his mind, the cause of the universal and the individual are identical.

We are not isolated and our uniqueness is not shattered by lack of private psychic life. All men meet in each man, yet every man is a unique centre of being, capable of maintaining his uniqueness if he is prepared to receive as well as to give. To reflect on the Eucharist is to see again the company of men in the lamplit room, it is not any meal on any occasion – there are stirrings of glory and stirrings of danger. The disciples are shortly to learn that without him they cannot bear one another; one of them finds that he cannot bear himself without his Master. In the shadow of the sacrifice of Christ we see the suicide of Judas. We see the poor distracted man shedding his own blood to atone for his own sins in contrast to the One who shed his Blood to redeem all men from the unbearableness of life without him in whom all creatures consist. There were stirrings of glory and stirrings of danger in the Upper Room. So there are at every Eucharist; the eucharistic food is the food for pilgrims. Our pilgrimage takes us into realms of life where we cannot always find words or images to describe what we see. Our pilgrimage takes us into realms of life where we see that both desires for visible security, tangible realities and a desperate clinging to what we understand are sinful. We know the point where we must abandon attempts at self-made security if we are to go on. Our pilgrimage brings us to fuller awareness that we are to think and pray and work as men whose most insignificant acts have consequences too wide to be measured by time or confined within the boundaries of a particular locality or of a particular group of people.

When the celebrant takes and blesses and breaks the bread, he is setting in motion a complexity of movements which go on and on affecting the whole existence of men and things until all comes to rest in the strange peace of God. Each communicant, of course, in co-operation with the celebrant, has his or her essential place in the cosmic, timeless acts. 'I am Alpha and Omega, saith the Lord, the beginning and the end.' Each Eucharist reminds us of our journey from God to God, and the eucharistic food is more than a remembrance that God sustains us throughout our journey; the eucharistic food is our sustenance. We can only talk about the mysteries of life by adding analogy to analogy, in God 'we live and move and have our being.' By the use of such language as this we do not deny the reality of this transitory world: bread and wine are frail creatures of time; our days are gone like a shadow, the time of our years is swifter than thought; but through our use of things impermanent God vouchsafes to us the permanent. Bread and wine, frail creatures of time, when blessed become the doors to timelessness. The Eucharist is the moment in and out of time.

I would end by making a soliloquy. The celebrant is one of the company who live in and out of time. His unworthiness is never the test of value of the Eucharist. His unworthiness can be a cloud between the people and God; a translucent cloud, but nevertheless a cloud. Sometimes the priest's unholiness is expressed in the minute blasphemy of littleness, of living in a small world bounded by parochial and domestic walls. Our pilgrimage lies across trackless stretches of barren land, where no water is and where no bird sings . . . across the distance the horizon calls; our plans for security – personal, domestic, parochial or diocesan – are then like scraps of paper whirled in the wind. Holiness is a matter of both size and order. The size and order of the celebrant's life is to be expressed in his voice, his movements and his silences in the sanctuary. Elsewhere it is to be seen in his compassion and in his firmness; in a gaiety devoid of frivolity; in a seriousness that is never grim; in hope that is quite distinct from secular optimism; in faith without sentimentality; in charity without dissimulation.

Let me conclude this soliloquy with words that are not mine:

A holy priest makes a fervent people;
A fervent priest, a pious people;
A pious priest, a decent people;
A decent priest, a godless people.

THE EUCHARIST: A MATTER OF LIFE AND DEATH

Jesus said, 'I am the way, the truth and the life'. Without the truth we perish; the way leads us to the desert and in life we know death, if not a physical death then a spiritual one, the kind of death a man may die before his body dies. No act of human will alone keeps a man alive –

> 'People who believe they are strong
> willed and masters of their destinies
> can only continue to believe this by
> becoming specialists in self-deception.
> Their decisions are not decisions at
> all . . . but elaborate systems . . .
> designed to make themselves and the
> world appear to be what they and the
> world are not! Spiritual death is
> an attempt to master the world and
> men; it is also an attempt to live
> outside the world of men. "Me,
> I want to escape . . . this dirty
> world, this dirty body, I never wish
> to make love again with anything more
> than the body." '

'In the midst of life we are in death' (Book of Common Prayer, Burial of the Dead), not the disintegration of the physical body but that more frightening disintegration of one who has ceased to believe in the significance of human action. 'Strait is the gate, and narrow is the way . . . and few there be that find it.' (Matthew 7 14) He who said this also breaks for us the Bread of Life, but he will not force us to eat.

No single statement can give a full explanation of the eucharistic activity (if such a statement could be made there would be no need for the sacrament). No series of propositional statements, formulae or parables will exhaust the mystery, every celebration is unique in that communicants have different experiences at each Eucharist. Our Lord said 'Do this in remembrance of me'. In the doing is the understanding; the activity is always more illuminating than mere pondering on its possible meanings. Like all human activity it begins in God, it is sustained and brought to its fulfilment but God does not act for human beings but with them. In the eucharistic action we bow before the unconsecrated bread to acknowledge our dependence on the ceaseless creative activity of God for bread to nourish our bodies and for truth to feed our minds and souls. We bow before the consecrated bread lost in wonder that we should be given the bread of life that others may be enriched and enlivened through us who are called to be the salt of the earth and the light of the world. This can be said because the eucharistic action is not a symbolic one but a participation in the life of a fellowship which has its being in God who loves earth and heaven with endless care.

The Eucharist can be thought of in numberless ways; one is suggested here. In the Eucharist we celebrate the glory of God and our mighty deliverance from fear of life through the saving acts of the Lord of life and death. To fear life is to be in a state of sin because it is a denial of the goodness of God and the splendour of men made in the image of God, destined to be free creative beings. Fear of living can bring about a kind of death. Wherever there can be death there can be a resurrection as seen in the life of one who is mastering fear in the adventure of living a human life.

Fear of life is shown in fear of action. One individual shrinks from action because it exposes him in its revelation of his scale of values and his lack of abilities. Another individual refrains from action on discovering that he can neither foresee nor control the process that his act initiates; such a person is ready to make acquaintanceships but not friendships; he will be an agreeable member of an institution but he will not accept office nor vote on any important issues. Individuals do not usually admit even to themselves that they are afraid to act, but they will postpone action till the moment for it is passed. They will plead insufficient time to think the matter over, or get the information necessary, or will claim exemption from responsibility on the grounds of indisposition. Groups fear action as the individuals who make up the group fear it. The committee will appoint a small sub-committee to report back with statistics to justify all findings. The more urgent the situation is, the more often it will be analysed and the more experts will be consulted. The Eucharist is not a preparation for action, it is an action in its own right. It can be said that it is a

rejoicing in the love of life made possible for us through him
who said of himself 'I am come that they might have life and
have it more abundantly.' No matter how much is said about
the Eucharist reference must be made to the necessity of
remembering that it is like a burst of applause made without
the main hope of benefiting oneself or others by this applause.
To use a Pauline phrase, the communicant is to be 'sorrowful
yet alway rejoicing'; he is to 'weep with those who weep and
rejoice with those who rejoice.' Only those who act significantly
are capable of tears and laughter. The inactive, the spiritually
dead, can neither weep nor rejoice. Those who fear life live as
little as possible, that is, they avoid overt action as much as
possible and even restrict the scope of their thinking. Yet at the
same time they fear inaction. Individuals feel that through
inaction their personal identity would dwindle (this feeling is
often found in both middle-aged and teenage delinquents) and
therefore, unconsciously, they magnify the importance of
existing obligations (family, work etc.) or they invent
obligations – A passes a periodical on to Z on Sundays and this
is done as if Z's life depended on receiving this periodical
(usually in such cases neither A nor Z reads it). Some
individuals bolster identity by membership of a great many
institutions and committees and find that through attendance
of many meetings their identity is established without the
burden of actions involving personal responsibility. There are
all sorts of further ways one can invent an identity for oneself
that is kept alive by finding others ready to join in this make-
believe; of course the process is largely unconscious and
seldom more than half-conscious. Groups (institutions, clubs,
committees etc.) also fear inaction because it could bring about
the end of the group's existence. For this reason a group will
set about, again largely unconsciously, the task of inventing
importance and the acts that maintain it. Importance is like
happiness – it eludes all who try to become important. The
wind bloweth where it listeth and some men are given
miraculous importance and the rest of us are illuminated
thereby. When churchmen (however selflessly) try to make the
church important in society the result is disaster. The mission of
the church is not to be important but to love God and to love the
world he loves. This love we understand through the Eucharist
which enables us to be ourselves partly by its constant

reminders of our own helplessness without God, of the apparent helplessness of the Lord of life and death in the hour of his crucifixion, and of the helplessness of the tomb to imprison him in death. Like importance, the ability to love must not be sought but recognised in the realisation of our connection with one another in God who breaks for us the bread of life not just once but again and again.

Participation in the eucharistic activity develops our knowledge of God and of ourselves. But this means that a man must overcome his fear of this twofold knowledge which is often first experienced as a knowledge of himself. Man hesitates to admit that he knows little about himself and so he attempts to limit his awareness of himself as much as possible in an effort to maintain control of himself. This limitation is a spiritual illness which ends in a kind of death to be described as an existence of boredom and banality in which nothing seems to happen. The adventurer, Christian or non-Christian, knows that the fullness of living, the excitement of living, begins in a willingness to increase his awareness of himself and continues through thinking and acting in accordance with his growing knowledge. The man who fears life fears mistakes; the adventurer accepts risks. Christians know this from frequent meditation on the twelve who sat at supper together in the Upper Room on Maundy Thursday night. If avoidance of mistakes and half-aliveness were more important than risk and adventure, the apostles would have been left in the familiar environment of the Galilean lakeside life with its drying nets and easy conversation about the size of catches, current prices and affairs of the little villages just off the quayside. Our Lord made it clear that these men were not called to be sinless but to be his disciples which continually put them in spiritual perils and dangers. St. Paul had this in mind when he wrote to first century communicants at Philippi and told them '. . . . Do all things without grumbling and questioning, that you may be blameless and innocent, children of God, without blemish, in the midst of a crooked and perverse generation, among whom you shine as lights in the world, holding fast the word of life . . .' This is not just giving a good example but living a life in which penitence and triumph are found. To shine as lights in the world means being fully alive. Communicants know the experience of shrinking back from this, preferring immediate comfort to the truth that sets men free.

Fear of living can bring about spiritual death. People can die this death through fear of being alone or through fear of being in a group. Some find solitude more bearable than company because, for one thing, they seem to be able to manage themselves better when they have not to deal with the unexpected in conversations and the complex effects people have on one another when they work or live together in groups. Group life is never easy and the more creative the group's work is, the more tension and conflict there will be within it; but groups who only talk about work being done (or left undone) by others can provide a temporary shelter for people who cannot face the full rigours of life in either solitude or society. The Fourth Gospel (like the other three Gospels), does not hide the difficulties in the life of the apostolic group and records our Lord's rejoicing that the twelve original members, with one exception, stayed with him till the end.

In all areas of life in this world it is easier for people to deal with enemies than with intimate friends and with rivals than with colleagues. These difficulties are expressions of the sin that is in us which threatens spiritual death to the individual and the groups to which he belongs. Christians are not immune from sin and sometimes even devoutness makes us harsh with one another and self-righteous about the world. But that is not all; the individual Christian and the group of Christians have their moments when they are caught up in the glory of God in the 'perfect love which casteth out fear.'

PRAYER

FUNDAMENTALS OF PRAYER

– Prayer, a significant activity –

Prayer is the most significant activity of men. It is a complex activity that brings into one all the activities of man. That means, for example, that a scientist is not to be thought of as one whose scientific works go on daily side by side with a separate activity called prayer, it is rather that his work in the laboratory is part of his praying and that scientific habits of thought have their effect on the way he prays. If the man of prayer is a scientist or a poet, he prays as a scientist or a poet. If he is an engineer or an artist or a salesman, he prays as an engineer or an artist or a salesman. If he is young or old or neurotic, he prays as one who is young or old or neurotic. Prayer is never to be used as an attempt to change what you are – it is always an attempt to be what you are as fully as you can by the grace of God.

– Prayer, an adventure –

Prayer is an adventure in thought, word and deed which leads men into an unknown territory and adventures they cannot control and the results of which they cannot foresee. All human knowledge is limited; a man does not know exactly what he is doing when he is praying, just as a poet does not know exactly what he is doing when he is writing poetry. A man of prayer and the poet will tell you that they do not altogether know how they pray or make poetry. To put this in another way, 'it is a terrible thing to fall into the hands of the living God' but not so terrible as to fall into the hands of men or into your own hands because 'your right hand can teach you terrible things.'

– Prayer, not definable –

There can be no absolute definition of prayer. To make such a definition would entail a complete knowledge of man, of God and of the whole universe. Descriptions of prayer can be, and are, made. There are special dangers whenever there is a tendency to limit thought about prayer by relying on one description alone; this single description is thus unconsciously turned into a definition. There are times that prayer should be examined in the interests of truth and love, but in the end prayer is to be practised rather than studied and talked about. The whole of an artist's life is not spent learning about brushwork and talking about other painters' pictures; he must paint his own pictures. In the same way, a man of prayer does not spend his life trying to find the most suitable way for him to pray and in discussions as to how other people pray. A painter cannot know himself apart from his paintings any more than a man of prayer can know himself apart from his praying.

– A man of prayer like an artist –

The man of prayer leads a certain style of life. Like the artist, he knows the moment of exaltation which vanishes before he realises fully its existence. In this case, his words cannot keep pace with the interplay of feelings and thoughts in this nameless exaltation. Such happenings are infrequent. The poet is known by the size and fullness of his wastepaper basket; the dusty pile of forgotten canvases is typical of the artist's studio; the man of prayer knows long hours spent feeling neither sorrow nor joy and almost no sense of reality. Like all creative workers, he knows the dread of wondering if his power to pray is slipping away from him, just as the painter can do nothing but stare at the empty canvas on his easel and the poet seems to himself as one who has lost both words and vision. In the whole of life, perhaps the most dreadful experience is to be like a sailing ship becalmed on the wide smoothness of the sea.

– Solitude and society –

Creative workers need a balance between solitude and society. A man who is not brave enough to bear being alone will not find himself, and hence will not find others no matter how much he involves himself with people. Artists and saints in their different ways have work to do which they can only do by being alone. Too much society, too much talking and too much movement combine to put a man out of touch with himself. The balance of society and solitude must be found and kept by each individual. In doing this, he must not lose sight of the value of each. For personal development we need silence but we also need communication with our fellows. It is never right to work against your temperament and the nature of your gifts and abilities. In our age, creative workers are tempted to give up the style of life which creative activity needs for a busyness in which the mood for their work is dispersed in the boredom and excitement of committees, conferences and commissions. Too many meetings and too much talking can blunt both sensibility and sensitivity. On the other hand, creative workers have to withstand the temptation common to many churchmen, that is, of attempting to leave the world that God loves, and to live in some privately made world which belongs neither to society nor church.

– The city –

Most of us are called to live out the Christian life of prayer in all the noise and bustle of a twentieth century city, where overcrowding, the rush of traffic leave one with very little opportunity of privacy, much less silence. This kind of life is more tolerable when one remembers that a city is part of God's creative work and a considerable human achievement, in that men took dust and water and out of these common substances made the vast cities that cover the world. To meditate on the wonder of cities can be just as apt as to meditate on the glory of the countryside, whose very shape owes much to the work of men, who drained swamps, altered the courses of rivers, quarried the mountainside and built a complex of roads. In fact, to seek God in the city is to seek him where he most truly is in the work of men who are the highest form of life we know. It is significant that the apex of our Lord's earthly ministry was reached in a city, the city of Jerusalem; it is also significant that Christianity flashed from city to city round the Mediterranean seaboard at remarkable speed.

– Silence and speech –

As well as solitude and society, the creative worker needs

both silence and speech, and happy is the household where speech is regarded as a luxury and silence as a necessity. Perhaps in our age we need to be sober in the use of speech, because we hear too many voices telling us too much about too many things and encouraging us to talk too much about our most significant work. It is difficult to explain but a man can talk himself out of his abilities and achievements. I mean that the poet or saint who tells too many people about how he versifies or how he prays is in danger of ceasing to be a poet or a man of prayer.

– Sorrowful and rejoicing –

The man of prayer does not make his ability to rejoice by forgetting the misery, pain and agony of men and women. In the words of St. Paul 'He is sorrowful yet alway rejoicing' and therefore can rejoice with those who rejoice and weep with those who weep. He maintains his joy by remembering frequently that a man's life does not consist in the abundance of his possessions, security, knowledge and education, and he does not merely remember this truth, he acts upon it, and in the school of action he learns how to abound and how to be in want. A man needs faith and courage to be joyful; he must risk being considered callous because he acts mindful that there are more things to do with life than preserve it; he insists that there are more important things than being healthy. Indeed, there is a sort of granite quality required of those who hold fast to the words of our Lord – 'Your joy no man taketh from you'. Joy is an element in a man's total life, it is expressed both directly and indirectly; it is probably seen most clearly in a person's response to those who rejoice and to those who are sorrowful.

– Worship –

The man of prayer is concerned with the joy of the church. Day by day, week by week, year by year the church rejoices in the birth, life, death, resurrection and ascension of Jesus Christ, whereby we are freed from the bondage of sin, death, time and the whole world order. We are exalted by exalting God, as Mary sang in the Magnificat 'My soul doth magnify the Lord . . . He that is mighty hath magnified me.' At every

Eucharist we celebrate the glory of God, who is all that is in all and we rejoice in our ability to participate in his creative activity. The taking and blessing and breaking of bread symbolises God's work and ours, for we do not celebrate this feast with him as paupers, pardoned criminals, slaves or servants. We celebrate the Eucharist as his sons and daughters.

– Who are 'we'? –

In the 1939-1945 war Archbishop Temple taught us to pray not as Englishmen who happened to be Christians but as Christians who happened to be Englishmen. This statement is capable of expansion; a philosopher does not pray as a philosopher who happens to be a Christian but as a Christian who happens to be a philosopher; he will enrich his prayer by his philosophizing. Philosophy and prayer are not contradictories but supplementaries. The mother of small children does not pray as a mother who happens to be a Christian but as a Christian who happens to be the mother of small children. This means that she will bring them up mindful that the whole of man's life is not taken up with fulfilling family obligations.

Who are we? In prayer, public or private, we use the word we, not to signify those who are praying together, not for all the usual local congregation. We use the pronoun we because we are the whole church making prayers and supplications and thanksgiving on behalf of all men. By birth we are made members of the human race, by baptism members of the Body of Christ; as church members we learn something of our responsibilities for our fellow-members and for all men singly and in groups.

– The church –
Where do you look for the church?

Where does a man look for the church in the world? He who keeps on searching eventually finds it. The search is not without shocks and disappointment. The searcher, perhaps half-consciously, expects to meet sinless mature people who do interesting and even exciting work in a rich and enriching fellowship with other church members. Instead he will find the counterparts of the first church members, the twelve Apostles. He will find a St. Peter whose impetuosity brings him to make quick promises and hasty denials; a St. Thomas who shrouds people with gloom and doubt; St. Peter, St. James and St. John who seem incapable of understanding another's needs in a complicated situation; the twelve Apostles running away from him at the first sign of danger; Judas, who betrayed his master for a few pounds; the twelve Apostles who even in the upper room argued hotly as to which of them should be the most important. The church is shaken by its members within and attacked by enemies from outside, and in various localities the church has disappeared.

If the searcher persists he will learn a lot about the church's belief in its existence from the form of worship with its due balance of praise, penitence and petition whenever the bread is broken, not only in remembrance of past act but in reverence for present fact that God is in all places and in all human activities. In worship, a man is lost in wonder, love and praise in which he finds himself in God by an effort which does not seem his own yet is really more his than all other acts.

– Joy in endurance –

It is joy to keep on holding that life is to be lived to the full whether one endures anxiety, disappointment, despair, betrayal or the terror of helplessness. 'Your joy no man taketh from you' but you have to keep it in the most testing conditions as well as when you have lost yourself in the joy of being alive. A man's life does not consist in having an easy path, an absence of conflict and temptation. Joy can be known in spite of conflict, anxiety, defeat and turmoil – this is symbolised by the Crown of thorns. The thorns stand for the agony of the Cross but the Crown stands for the unconquerable King who for the joy that was set before Him endured the Cross, despising the shame, and has sat down at the right hand of the throne of God.

– The sins of individuals –

In the course of rejoicing, a man sometimes sees himself and feels constrained to confess his sins, not to man but to God.

What does he want to confess? Often, certain of his thoughts, words and deeds appal him; more frequently, it is his common state of soul that seems the sin. He sees his general life as shabby, trivial, anxious, boring others and boring himself; this is the style of life a person lives who doubts the significance of human behaviour and consequently avoids accepting responsibility and will not commit himself as long as he can avoid doing so. Or, he may feel that he has not the integrity of a hero or a martyr; on the contrary, his timidity frightens him and makes it difficult for him and for others to pray.

– The sins of groups –

When a Christian examines himself, he finds that he is indirectly guilty on account of what is happening in the various groups to which he belongs; he makes and is made by this constellation of groups. The members of his family may be anxious to protect one another from life rather than encourage one another to run the risks of love and living. Clubs, societies, and so on, provide many occasions for temptation, but the Christian is called not to run from temptations which are inevitable but to learn how to deal with them. A group has a life of its own which cannot be entirely controlled by its members and therefore men are often entangled with sins they neither know nor understand. It is a mystery but no one acts alone – the sin of one is a sin of all, just as the prayer of one is a prayer of all. A Christian finds himself bearing both the sorrows and the joys of all men. Because this is so, whenever a man prays in private or in public he naturally uses the plural pronoun 'we' for we are all wrapped up together in the bundle of life.

– Forgiveness –

How does a man know when he is forgiven? There is no way except by acting as if forgiven. He then finds that he is. There should be no asking for special signs or special feelings. There is no special sign except the signs that he finds in the course of activity. The more deeply a man lives the more deeply he is tempted and he cannot always resist temptation. The very love he expresses can be almost his undoing. The practice of our religion exposes a person to spiritual dangers more serious than any dangers encountered by those who choose a safe life, that is, a life without love or hate, without large acts. It cannot be said too often that Christianity is not a way to escape sin, a consolation or a way of securing yourself against all accidents.

– Preoccupation with sin –

In both private and public prayer it is important that confession is kept in proportion, that is to say, an unduly large part of the prayers should not be concerned with sin and forgiveness. The main object of Christian prayer is not to confess sins but to know God and rejoice in his majesty, power and dominion. Without denying the terrors of sin, the vision of God must always come first. Perhaps the most serious sin can be described as a failure to see God and your neighbour and yourself in the ceaseless movement of life.

– Confession –

Confession is made up of the sins a man is conscious of committing in thought, word or deed and in the sins he shares with fellow-members of the groups to which he belongs. His confession is really incomplete if he is not bearing sins not only his but man's. We are all bound up together by our birth and by our baptism: we are members one of another; when one sins, all sin. When one confesses, all confess, but how far can we say that all are forgiven?

– Intercession –

The man of prayer cannot spend the greater part of every day in making specific acts of prayer; his prayer time is limited and he must carefully guard himself from the tendency to overcrowd his prayers with intercession; he can easily get his prayers out of balance and blame himself. Many find the lists of individuals and causes using up too much energy and time and yet they feel afraid to shorten the number of intercessions which seem to be necessary. One cannot imagine prayer, public or private, without intercession but we know that too many intercessions can stifle us, especially when lists give all sorts of detailed information. If prayer is to be prayer, its proper

activity must be clearly guarded. The primary object of prayer is
to know God, not in a selfish, exclusive way but as the Father of
all who knows our intercessions before we make them.

– Immediacy of intercession –

Our intercessions should be concerned with those who are
nearest to us, that is, it would be unnatural not to intercede for
fellow church-members, family, friends, people we work with
daily. In thinking of them, often action is the best kind of
intercession. It is better to pray for the peace of an office by
doing peaceful things such as not banging doors and talking
too much to colleagues who are preoccupied; that is to say,
doing the appropriate things to make your office or family life a
reasonable and joyful one. Sometimes it is easier to pray for
people in Africa and India rather than for those you see
continually and daily.

– Intercession and the goodness of God –

Tendencies to bargain with God should be checked, for
example, 'I know that X has done no work for his examination
but please make it that he passes and if he does I'll pray more
often'. Frequently this pagan notion comes into prayer, that is,
we desire to find a way to make God work for us – 'not thy will
but mine be done'.

– Intercession and purpose –

In making intercessions we are to be clear as to what we want
most for those for whom we pray. First and foremost, we wish
every individual to be himself and no other person and
therefore we pray not that a situation will be made for him but
that he may be strong enough to bear the burdens that
responsibilities thrust upon him. We do not pray that people
may be kept away from enemies and temptations, we pray
rather that they may be able to withstand enemies and
overcome temptations. In making intercessions we must be
quite clear that death and sickness are not the worst things that
can happen to a man. We do not want to pray that we may be
delivered from trouble, rather we should build one another up

for greatness: Jesus says 'Seek ye first the Kingdom of Heaven and all these things shall be added unto you'. What things? – the things you need for faith and the ability to see, hope and the power of understanding, love and the humility to speak and act, or watch and wait, till the situation's movement guides you to play your part. As in life, as in drama, greatness lies in timing the entrance and the action. The Christian is called to be greater than the one-virtue man; that is, greater than the man who is, for example, patient in all situations whether patience is the appropriate response or not. The gospels make it clear that the hands of Jesus which blessed little children were the hands that overthrew the tables of the money-changers and merchants in the Court of the Gentiles.

– Persistence –

The Sermon on the Mount advises persistence in prayer . . . keep on asking and you will receive, keep on searching and you shall find, keep on knocking and it shall be opened to you. Ask and you will receive – you will discover the questions you should ask – this is not to put your petition in the form of asking God to give you the solution of your problem, you will be given sufficient understanding of what your problem is. Seek and ye shall find. Where to seek and how to seek, that is, a scientist in his examination of matter and space finds more of himself and of connections with men and things. In general any honest man who loves his neighbour begins to understand himself in them more and more. Keep on knocking and it will be opened whichever side you are on, that is, you may be a prisoner bound fast in narrowness of mind or through making too many commitments.

A MEDITATION ON THE THEOLOGY OF PRAYER

1. *Faith and Knowledge*

The great human questions – what am I? What am I to do? Am I my brother's keeper? Is he mine? Does it matter what I do? – drive us to despair or prayer.

Now we know in part, but fragmentary knowledge is real knowledge.

We walk by faith, not by sight. For St. Paul the opposite of faith is not doubt but sight. That is, we walk by faith and knowledge but depend more on faith than on knowledge. Faith and knowledge grow up together and nourish one another.

Every time I say: 'I believe in God' I make an affirmation that I am a being capable of making an act of faith.

Theology is not a subject to be studied but a discipline which entails the maintenance of a special way of thinking, speaking and acting. Bishop Westcott held that theology is only pure when it is applied. In other words, we do not theologise about theology but we think theologically about all men and all things.

Theology normally begins in prayer, continues in thought and ends in prayer.

Theology shows that individuals and things cannot be understood in isolation but must be looked at in their context.

Prayer cannot be considered apart from the individual, the church and the world.

No scientist would be ready to give a literal description of the universe. No theologian should be ready to describe exactly what happens when a man prays. To give a literal description we would need to know all about the world of men and how God deals with it.

2. *The World and the Church*

What am I doing when I am praying? It is well not to be too curious. No man can think and pray at the same time and do both well.

What we do when we are not praying shapes what we do when we pray. What we do when we are praying shapes what we do when we are not praying. Theology safeguards these facts with its emphasis on man's responsibility for his actions.

Individuals, the world and the church live and move and have their being in God.

I do not believe in God because I believe in the world; I believe in the world because I believe in God who loves the world. I do not believe in God because I believe in the church; I believe in the church because I believe in God. I believe in the world and the church because I am sure that in them God provides the situation in which a man may be a man.

When I pray for the church and the world I find that I am praying for myself, and when I pray for myself I find I am praying for the world and the church.

'Those whom God hath joined together let no man put asunder.' The individual, the world and the church are one in God.

In God all things have their origin; he is to be thought of as the maker of words, bread, wine and prayers – all our operations are co-operations with him, and though the help we give him is fragmentary we know that fragmentary help is real help.

3. General Reflections

The theology of prayer does not tell me exactly what I am doing when I pray but tells me how to think of what I am doing when I pray.

Prayer is stillness, quietness, movement, sometimes depending on a form of words or a single word, or a mood which is more easily recognised than described. Prayer is a creative activity because it gives a person power and peace and vision. While prayer begins by paying attention to some particular thing or person it may end in starting a process beyond human control.

A conversation can turn into prayer in the form of a dialogue.

In public worship, worshippers are ministers of grace to one another. A man needs both solitude and society if he is to live fully. The one who is too solitary becomes distorted; the one who is too social is in danger of becoming busy and empty.

Both public and private worship are hard, and few there be who bear the hardship.

Prayer may be called: a relationship that includes all relationships; a longing for the experience that includes all experiences; a realization that the knower, the known and the knowing are one; an adventure that takes me into mysterious parts of my being. Prayer may be called an expansion of my self-awareness which is another way of describing the feeling of having found God in myself and myself in him.

We must never be worried if we pray badly; it is better to pray badly than not to pray at all.

We must learn not to measure spiritual happenings by the clock. A person's most important experience may all be over in the flash of a second but the afterglow remains.

Our prayers will often disturb us, as through them we see more clearly the obligations consequent upon our relations with other people.

We find life rushed, noisy, never free from movement. If we are to remain spiritually alive we need determination and skill to train ourselves to be flexible, that is, to turn from work to prayer and back again without the work suffering from lack of concentration or the prayer becoming mechanical. It is not that the Christian is to leave people and the world to pray and be holy; he is to be holy wherever he is in the noise and disturbance of modern conditions.

Often prayer disturbs us by revealing to us that Christians are called not to goodness but to greatness.

4. *Summary*

Jesus said: 'When you pray, go into your room and shut the door and pray to your Father who is in secret; and your Father who sees in secret will reward you'.

God became man without ceasing to be God that men might be godly without ceasing to be men.

PIETY[1]

It is dangerous to talk and think too much about the possession of any virtue, for virtue is not an end in itself; it is not acquired but is received as a gift by those who are more interested in being disciples than in receiving rewards. We are to consider the virtue of piety. It is not possible to say a great deal about it directly but much can be said about it indirectly. Piety is a by-product of the constant attempt a Christian makes to love God, his neighbour, and himself, in thought, word, and deed. His love of God begins in God who gives to each person the power to love and who ceaselessly makes the visible and invisible things which stimulate and nourish this love. The devout man, therefore, does not clamour for virtues but desires knowledge and power to love as he is loved. This knowledge and power are given him as he cares for things and people. To put this in another way, our love for God begins and develops in our love of things and people whose very being is in God, for he is in our eyes and in our looking just as he is in what we behold.

Berdyaev says somewhere that a Christian should be ready to risk even his own soul for love of the brethren. No doubt this is an extravagant statement but perhaps nearer the truth about piety than the picture of one wrapping himself up carefully to preserve his good character. This picture becomes quite ludicrous when put beside authentic Christian images of piety such as the judgement story of Matthew, chapter 25. In this story the blessed ones exclaim in surprise: 'Lord, when saw we thee an hungered, and fed thee? or thirsty, and gave thee drink? When saw we thee a stranger, and took thee in? . . .' The blessed ones performed works of mercy quite unaware of themselves as doing anything important, in complete contrast to those depicted in Matthew, chapter 7, as blusteringly demanding notice: 'Lord, Lord, have we not prophesied in thy name? and in thy name have cast out devils? and in thy name done many wonderful works?' To them the Lord replies: 'I never knew you: Depart from me, ye that work iniquity.' From these images it would seem that spontaneous generosity and

---

[1]   First published in *Theology* 1962 and reprinted in *Traditional Virtues Reassessed* ed. A. R. Vidler, S.P.C.K. 1964.

an unawareness of doing good to others are fundamental
marks of piety. No one can teach or learn spontaneity and
unawareness of self in doing good as one might teach or learn
a subject like algebra. It is dangerous to long secretly, or to
encourage others to long secretly, for spontaneity and
unselfconsciousness in dealing with people. To desire such
things is to push them out of one's reach or to manufacture
their counterfeits with the help of like-minded associates.

A pious man's acts cannot be understood apart from the man
himself and the circumstances in which they are performed.
Piety is not mechanical obedience to a code. Piety is to be
described rather than explained; it is not so much defined as
recognized in a pious man's expressions of love for things and
people. His love of things is not a sentimental regard for them
but a desire to understand them and use them rightly. This
approach to creatures leads him to wonder and marvel at the
mystery of God's creation as manifested in both countryside
and city. The stars in the sky and the neon-lit city alike proclaim
the greatness of God, and the greatness of the power he gives
to men. But the invisible created things are even more
wonderful than the visible. Who can cease to be amazed at the
speed of thought and the rich unexpectedness of imagination?
How can the sharpness of intelligence be described? What is
more wonderful than the response men make to music? What is
more remarkable than the enlargement of consciousness
brought about through giving attention to poetry, drama, or
painting? The Christian turns his mind towards these invisible
things and finds God in them, or rather is found by God in
them. Everything begins in God who is the source of all that is
or ever shall be. But more wonderful than all visible or invisible
things is that strange peace of God which is given together
with the sense of having seen, as it were, the shadow of the
Creator reflected by created things.

Everything we know about the pious man shows us that we
must not be obsessed with visible or invisible things lest we
cease to pay proper attention to people. People are the highest
kind of created life we know, and through them we are led to a
deeper knowledge of ourselves and of God who commands us
to love one another. Love of one another, of course, entails the
performance of the gospel deeds of mercy, which are different
for every generation. In our generation in this country the

common poverty is spiritual rather than material; that is to say, the bulk of people are poor in ideas, interests, and in spiritual means of using the freedom that the present type of society offers them. There is no need to stress the difficulty of this kind of ministration. At the same time we are faced with finding the right way to help the millions of people in other parts of the world who are destitute, homeless, and oppressed, knowing that all we can do is to take what political action we can and subscribe towards the alleviation of this widespread poverty. This knowledge weighs heavily upon us and it should not be banished from the mind, but the devout know the danger of neglecting immediate and difficult obligations through too much concern with violence, injustice, and starvation in far-away places. The New Testament always shows our Lord giving close attention to those who are in his company. In looking at this attention people learn what it means to be with him and to be with one another. In his life 'with' means far more than being physically near. It means the closeness of a unity which love makes by serving others and accepting the service of others. Our Lord showed this truth most vividly when he took up a towel and basin and washed his disciples' feet, and when he allowed the woman to wash his feet at supper in Bethany. Further, these two incidents are also concrete statements of what is implied by his words: 'It is more blessed to give than to receive.' It is blessed to receive but it is more blessed to give. Happy are we when someone receives what we offer and when we are enriched by accepting what we are offered. Human relationships cannot be described merely as a giving and receiving of material things because there is also a subtle giving and receiving of invisible things. We nourish one another not by presenting a good example but in the way our Lord implies when he says: 'Ye are the salt of the earth . . . Ye are the light of the world. . . . . . Let your light so shine before men, that they may see your good works, and glorify your father which is in heaven.' We are not to wave the light to attract men's attention nor hide it from their possible scorn: we are to let it shine. This is the most difficult work in the world and can be done only by those who are being freed from anxiety about their own devoutness and their influence over others.

Perhaps what we do for others is done largely in their

absence, for in their absence we make and maintain the interior dispositions which determine how we act in those common situations for which there can be no particular preparation. In the absence of others the Christian makes two kinds of reflection. First, the general reflection on what it is to be man according to the gospel, and secondly, on those people for whom he has an immediate concern. The Gospels underline the value of each person as a unique being made in the image of God, and therefore each person is to be reverenced no matter how degraded he may be. This reverence for humanity guides every pious man's concern for his neighbour, just as it informs the priest's pastoral and evangelistic ministrations; it is also shown by Christian artists, writers, and dramatists in their care to treat human beings as responsible for the quality of life they live. In our complex and rapidly changing society we are driven to give a great deal of thought to relationships. A relationship can be a prison or an escape from fullness of living. Relationships are important but they become disastrous if treated as ends in themselves. Our Lord spoke about this when he told the disciples: 'Think not that I am come to send peace on earth: I came not to send peace, but a sword. For I am come to set a man at variance against his father . . . And a man's foes shall be they of his own household. He that loveth father or mother more than me, is not worthy of me . . .' That is, a disciple is not to cease loving his fellows or to spurn relationships, but he is to lead the style of life which is generated and shaped by loving God more than his fellows and his relationships.

Inevitably general reflection about people leads to the second type of reflection – the particular thought given to those with whom one has immediate contact. Reverence for them is to be preserved by its relevant expression in the rush and bustle of everyday living. Negatively, this reverence is first to avoid the temptation to dominate another even for his own good, and secondly the refusal to foist a role on him by suggesting what his feelings, ambitions, or amusements should be. At the same time the devout must be alert lest they allow anyone to dominate them or be found even temporarily accepting a false role. Positively, reverence for others is expressed by doing all one can to provide the kind of conditions which seem to give them the best chance of being truly themselves. In Christian terms this means doing nothing that makes it difficult for others to pray (among other things, to avoid talking too much, to allow people enough solitude, and yet to be aware when they need company). Pious people, of course, do not narrow prayer down to a series of acts performed at intervals, but rather consider it a state of mind and soul which is formed by and forms direct acts of public and private prayer. Christians know how easy it is to break up this inner state of devoutness; a hasty outburst, a word, a look, the slamming of a door, the over-hearty greeting, the animated discussion of trivialities – such things can test a man's inner poise at times too severely for his endurance. Usually on big occasions most of us behave tolerably well, but on little occasions piety is tested by the people one meets and works with day by day. This is so because the bulk of people, while truthful and honest in their dealings over material things, have little regard for the hidden struggles of those who want to think, speak, do, and be the truth. Intercession for the sanctity of others is best expressed in overt acts that are judged to promote it in given situations. Ascetic discipline is most truly to be found in the constant attempt to avoid disturbing and distracting our neighbours, and particularly our nearest neighbours, by the disorderliness of our behaviour and our dullness in perceiving the succession of their moods.

As the last paragraph shows, thought about others leads to a consideration of prayer; this is always the case in a Christian's thinking because all thinking begins in God and can only find its fulfilment in him. The pious man knows that meditation on anything or any person can result in his being drawn into prayer, because to pay attention to any of God's creatures is to be found by God through the mediation of the creature. But one needs to add that a Christian must deliberately give his attention to specifically Christian subjects if his prayer is not to degenerate into sentimental pantheism or humanist musings that are no more than musings. The foundation of Christian prayer must be meditation on the gospel images; for God, though not confined by the limits of any image, is its life just as he is the life of the meditation a man makes. A man's meditation is not to be devoted to one image alone – which would be self-imprisonment – nor must he ever forget that the totality of these images at best reveals no more than glimpses of him who is the ground of their being. It is always wise, we are taught, to speak little about prayer but to give much attention to the things that make prayer possible.

One of these things, specially for our generation, is the development of flexibility of mind. Von Hügel describes this flexibility as an ability to move from prayer to work and from work back to prayer without the work becoming inefficient or the prayer mechanical. This is a particularly important skill to practice in a society where there is little leisure and little solitude for those who wish to pray. The pious man now is noted not necessarily for the length of time he spends in prayer but for this flexibility which is made possible by his power to work and to enjoy himself without being over-absorbed in what he is doing. Or, to put it in another way, he lives lightly and does not become heavily earnest even in his most important occupations. This way of living is not learnt from text-books and is best considered as the grace given to those who are attempting to live in the light of the Lord's injunction: 'Be not anxious . . .' Faith results in a carefreeness which may look very like carelessness or callousness to an uninitiated observer. Often the pious fail because they overburden themselves with goodness. In prayer this overburdening is either the result of a rule of life which demands more time directly given to prayer than the fulfilment of obvious obligation allows, or of a weight of intercessions which can turn what could be prayer into a feat of memory or a feeling of guilt at inability to pray for so many people and causes. Rules of life and intercession lists need a great deal of attention in the light of the doctrinal assumptions of those who suggest the rules and lists and of those who accept them. But woe to us if we think the Christian life can be lived without order. Woe to us if we intercede unwisely. Woe to us if we cease to pray for others.

Private prayer cannot be considered apart from thoughtful, devout, and imaginative preparation for and participation in public worship. Christians do not doubt that public worship is the Church's main corporate action. But many doubt the place and value of some of the Church's weekday actions other than the daily offices, confirmation preparation, marriage interviews, hearing confessions, and the like. This doubt is an act of love and loyalty; it comes into consciousness whenever a Church project seems unnecessary, impossible, or only to be understood as at attempt to interest some individual or to keep members together by performing a common task. The church community and its members only grow to maturity through attempting to do what is both necessary and possible in a society which makes it increasingly difficult to keep on believing in the significance of human action. The whole question of human action in the world is tolerable for those who believe that the world lives and moves and has its being in God who sent his son not to condemn the world but to save it. The life of the devout, therefore, is an active response to a call to be the salt of the earth and the light of the world. This is not a calling to be sinless but to lead a particular style of life which is given the name pious. To be pious is to have a strong realization of one's share in the guilt of all men as well as to bear the burden of one's own wrongdoings. But penitence and piety are not interchangeable terms. The pious man is to be as capable of rejoicing with them that rejoice as he is of weeping with them that weep; he is to be sorrowful yet always rejoicing; he is to be as wise as a serpent and as harmless as a dove. Though poor he is to make many rich, because those who receive a pious man in the name of a pious man shall receive a pious man's reward.

PRAYER AS TALKING TO GOD

He came to his own home, and his own people
received him not. But to all who received him, who
believed in his name, he gave power to become children
of God.

JOHN 1 11-12

'When you pray say – Our Father . . .'

LUKE 11 2

Prayer begins with an urge to find or to be in touch with the
great power which makes all in all and yet whose being seems
outside and beyond all. Christianity says that prayer is a man's
response to the presence of God who calls him through all
things and all men, because God is all that is in thing or man.

Prayer can be described in many ways: here are two of them –
prayer is talking to God; prayer is thinking about God. To
consider the first of these descriptions: the image for prayer is
not a pair of clumsy hands stretched out beyond oneself in an
attempt to grasp something beyond reach; the image for
prayer is not an attempt to jump out of oneself into the life of
the other. Prayer consists in being ourselves most fully and so
finding God in ourselves and ourselves in God. Prayer begins
in an attempt to be conscious of ourselves and gradually
enlarging our awareness of all that we are connected with; and
this enlargement of ourselves is part and parcel of what we
speak of as talking to God.

Prayer is talking to God, that is, prayer is talking to a person
(for we are told to say Our Father when we pray). We only
become persons by talking with persons, but talking, to be
really talking, must be about a subject and that subject will be
constantly developing and changing. But we should
remember that in the end all talking is about persons because
there could be no subject for conversation without the activities
of persons. One goes further and says that in the end all talking
is talking about God for without him there could be neither
thought nor word nor movement of any sort. We are now
specially thinking of prayer as talking to God. Most of us find
in our prayers that we want to talk a lot about people,
particularly individuals and groups of individuals because

thought about anyone inevitably means consideration of the
various groups to which he belongs. Most of us want to talk
about those for whom we have direct responsibility in church,
work, friendship, family life. When we talk about them in
prayer to God we, as it were, make a mood (or a state of mind)
where we see more clearly what those we pray for really need,
and what we are to do for them and what we cannot do for
them. We know that each person needs such things as we can
give by making the conditions through which he may become
a fully developed person. For this reason we realise that every
group should allow sufficient freedom to its members for each
to be a man. In talking to God in prayer about people we see
the difference between living competently and efficiently and
living creatively and dangerously. We see that parents have
done their work for their children when their sons and
daughters become independent of them. We see that teachers
will want pupils to love the truth in spite of the hard demands
of knowledge and the sorrow which it brings. We see that
friends will want each to love life more than happiness or even
peace. When a man talks to God in prayer he gets to know
himself better and in getting to know himself more widely and
deeply he increases in his knowledge of God. This is not in the
sense of knowing all about God and all things and all men but
knowledge in the sense of knowing a person; we know people,
and some of them extremely well, but we do not know all about
anybody and sometimes man is alarmed to discover how little
he knows about himself. Christianity says that no-one can
completely know himself and this complete knowledge
belongs to God alone. In prayer, by the Grace of God, men and
women increase in wisdom and stature and in favour with God
and man, not in favour with all men but with all who belong to
the household of faith.

PRAYER AS THINKING OF GOD

In the beginning was the Word . . . And the
Word became flesh, and dwelt among us full
of grace and truth; we have beheld his glory,
glory as of the only Son from the Father.

JOHN 1 1 & 14

You shall not make yourself a graven image.

EXODUS 20 4

God became man without ceasing to be God
that men might be godly without ceasing
to be men.

ST ANSELM

It can be said that prayer is talking to God and prayer is
thinking about God. To consider prayer as thinking about God
– it can be further described as thinking godly thoughts about
oneself and the whole world of things and men which, of
course, is inevitable in our desire to think about God who is the
subject of all our thinking and the light by which we think. In
other words a good deal of prayer consists in thinking the
greatest thoughts about God and about oneself. In our
maturity we see the difficulties and pain in doing this because
we must reconcile ourselves to tornadoes, typhoons, the
devastation of a whole countryside when rivers burst their
banks. We have to reconcile ourselves to the brutality, the
treachery and the pitiable weakness of all sorts of men. Such
things must be in our thinking about God, and much Christian
devoutness consists in bearing the burden of being man in
dark and bitter surroundings, as well as in the realms of joy and
peace growing out of a faith that is more than belief in the
existence of a being beyond all we know. Faith must go on in
spite of fragmentary knowledge and inability to understand all
the results of action, and go on in spite of being hurt by what
men do to one another in the name of love or at the prompting
of fear or greed. This human position would be unbearable
without the deliberate and open manifestation of God in the
Word made flesh Who thus leads us into a maturity which is
able to bear both human sorrows and joys, and makes us

capable of recognising that submission to circumstances is the beginning of our understanding of them and the exercise of our powers in them.

Christians, of course, in thinking about God cannot and do not want to banish the images of the Gospels out of their minds. And considering the gospel images it is to be remembered that it is disaster if one keeps a single image fixed and pays insufficient attention to the other images in the mind. The Jewish commandment says thou shalt not make to thyself any graven image. With that in mind it might be said that thou shalt not make to thyself any fixed mental image. Bearing this in mind we remember that prayer (and the whole life of a Christian) is fed by images.

In prayer and in all mental life thought is the most important kind of deed. To a large extent we are made by thinking and we make others by thinking, therefore it matters a great deal what we think about and how we think; nowhere is this more important than when we pray and therefore in our prayers we want to enlarge ourselves through spreading wide the gate of our attention to all the images. Beside the crucified figure we have to put the wedding guest; beside the image of the stable we must put the figure of the shepherd; beside the man with the scourge in his hand, advancing on the traders and the money-changers, we must put the figure of him laying his hands on little children to bless them. Beside the figure of desolation in Gethsemane we must put the man who denounces the wolves in sharp biting words, while at the same time he wept for Jerusalem. We may fasten our attention on the movement of his hands which healed the sick; these are strong hands, hands grown flexible and hard through work at the carpenter's bench, these are the hands which were broken and pierced by nails hammered in by a Roman soldier who neither knew nor cared about what he was doing. We look at the man bound with chains in Pilate's presence and we know which of the two had power.

He said to the disciples: 'I am not come to send peace but a sword.' He also said: 'I am the bread of life . . . Come to me all who labour and are heavy laden and I will give you rest . . . Marvel not that the world hates you for it hated me before it hated you.' We could go on and on multiplying the images of the Gospel. We know that no single one will do; we know that the selection of a small number of them will not do either; we know that even taking them all together would still only succeed in giving indications of a possible image which could show all that could be shown about him. But no such image exists or could exist. We are blest by our use of images and the blessing lies in showing us how to think of the being that cannot be represented truly by one single image or any group of images. He is the life in all things, and to us he seems to move in things and men and outside them at the same time but he vouchsafes to us a larger knowledge of his being than images alone could ever give us.

LOVE IN THE WORLD

Christian Community [1]

The dangers of collectivism are always near, frequently incurred. The Bible analogy of shepherd and sheep is turned into an allegory instead of being left as an analogy. Sheep are too gregarious and too docile to be taken as 'standing for' the people. The analogy is only concerned with the responsibility of shepherds. A great number of heartbreaking pastoral talks are given on the assumption (unexamined) that the people respond singly and behave gregariously as sheep do. Note the Gospel emphasis: a man prepared to die for the Truth is not the sort of person who is easily led; at any rate the response of sheep is far too forseeable and automatic to be any use for the understanding of people. Our pastoral task is not confined to the sheeplike.

The present parochial system is based on an assumption which can no longer be made. In fact the Church of England is more and more 'congregational' than 'parochial'. This is largely due to the shifting population and modern transport, together with the different varieties of Anglicanism. Further there are parish churches which, for reasons other than churchmanship, are not places where people find they can worship. I know this is not new to the thought of either of us, but rather a theme which recurs again and again. Should the Church of England behave as if it were a monster institution or a minority group in a kindly tolerant community? Behind all that we have to ask, can one expect Christianity to be a thing capable of drawing the masses of people into the Body of Christ?

How are we to take 'the strait gate and the narrow path, and few there be that find it'? The Church bears the burden of all humanity's sins and the exultation of humanity's achievements. I think a good deal of work has been done on the 'world' (a) not to confuse the world and the wicked world, and (b) to be quite clear that we love the world (which means clear-sightedness of its good and evil – we are to rejoice, for instance,

---

[1] Extract from a private letter to a priest.

in the discovery and use of electricity and in works of art whether the work of churchmen or not), (c) to meditate on the connection between church and world, beginning with reflection on the fact that (i) both church and world live and move and have their being in God, and (ii) by birth and by baptism each churchman is inescapably caught and held in the action and interaction of church and world. By birth and living an atheist is affected by the church in all sorts of oblique ways. I think that the way one reacts to this paragraph is expressed in pastoral and evangelistic work.

Many, and I think most, serious parochial clergy are questioning the system to their pain, but in the name of truth. I think this is a most difficult time for priests – a sort of corporate 'dark night' in which the church, where it is strong, is watchful and patient rather than bursting into activities in response to 'invented needs'. Profound alterations in church life more often come not so much for straight doctrinal reasons as in response to so-called 'secular happenings', for example, the cost of fuel rising and rising, the younger average age of marriage, and so on; when this is recognised and dealt with considerable changes in church life result. In the meantime, we priests are very much to be watchmen, to be those who leave minds open enough to make the attempt to read the signs of the times.

In every age the church has divided into units for worship: the make-up of these units is sometimes geographical, sometimes occupational or professional. Our problem now is to look carefully at the way worshipping units come together now that the geographical structure of parishes has almost gone, leaving us the task of looking after these units. In time these units may grow smaller in membership while multiplying in the total number of groups. We are unsettled through the breaking up of regional groups in cities and rural areas. The grouping of people is a bit of a scientific study; you cannot drag people together in parish or building estate (I mean new housing estate!) by putting them down beside each other, believing that fusion comes purely by juxtaposition. Priests, I think, could do a great deal by contacts with all sorts of people who are NOT their parishioners.

Join me in these my present ponderings: the church looked at as an institution; the things which go to enrich an institution; the confict, often unconscious, between institutions in the community; the church's attitude towards other institutions.

Tillich says in one of his sermons, 'to see is to share'. Seeing is sharing. Seeing and sharing do not happen separately but at the same time. In a parish there are all sorts of people, all sorts of complex relationships within the parish group, so that it is some time before a new incumbent knows the pulls and tugs and pushes that buffet him about. Much of this is all unconsciously going on and goes on through the deliberate action of the group. Is it not awfully hard to know what is happening in any group? We do not know what we do, or rather we have only a fragmentary knowledge of what we do.

ON BEING BORN: THE VOCATION TO BE HUMAN

'It is easy to be a saint, if you
have not got to bother about being
human.'

'Early sense of life is lost in
manhood. Originally it is neither
selfish nor unselfish, it joins
the self to what is around.'

One step towards the full establishment of the Christian
doctrine of man is to take birth seriously. To be born, of course,
means to be born in sin, but that is only one aspect of the truth
about man. The fact of being born has a multiplicity of
ramifications which are to be traced out if our thinking about
man, baptism, the church and society are to provide us with
concepts of realities.

The baptised are not bidden to forget that they are human,
rather they are bidden in their baptism to learn to be human.
Care must be taken that the baptised are not exposed to the
dangers manufactured by those who have misunderstood
what the spiritual doctors say about inordinate love of
creatures. This misunderstanding leads to a value being placed
upon man's development as an isolated individual; this
elementary error cannot be corrected by adding zealous
exhortations about social responsibility. The misunderstanding
is evidence of another case of theological schizophrenia. A
serious study, for example, of Dom Butler's 'Western
Mysticism' and a continuance of the thought and study which
such a work prompts, would correct many of the current false
impressions accepted and given about the devotional life of the
baptised. A great deal of thought needs to be given to
corporate and private intercessory prayer. The content in much
intercessory prayer divides sharply into those who pray and
those are are prayed for, thus completely disregarding the
metaphysical connection made between men by birth. There is
lack of both humanity and Christianity whenever we take up an
attitude of the fortunate pitying the unfortunate and praying
for them. The greatest is the servant of all, and the kind of
service implied is not one that divides but uncovers the

fundamental unity of all men.

Many still go to church as an act of individual piety; and the Anglican attitude even to communicants is mixed. There is much said about corporateness which is not in line with the little manuals of devotion recommended and given to communicants in many cases. The escape from individualism in church is not made easy by the varying connotation given to the pronoun 'We' as it is used in the course of public worship. 'We' as used both in and out of the pulpit so often means 'We, the English people' and not 'We, the members of the Body of Christ.' The unhappy choice of prayers after the Third Collect further complicates the worshipper's clarity when he is led to think of himself successively as (a) one of those present in this church now, (b) an Englishman, (c) a member of a certain parish, (d) a member of some organisation, (e.g. Boy Scouts), (e) a citizen of Middletown. Unless clearness is expressed about group-membership in church worship, how can the Christian be given advice about the conduct of his life which can only be understood where group loyalties are recognised and arranged in a scale of descending importance?

There is much need of co-operation between liturgiologists and moral theologians: the former to go on and on expounding what the pronoun 'We' means when it is used in Church, the latter to work out the Christian's duty in the light of his membership of so many groups. There is need for a new expression of what it means to be honest, not so much in regard to material things, but in the realms of human relationships where so many are concerned to know what is treachery and what is not treachery in our contemporary society. Look, for example, at the miner with his double loyalty to Trade Union and to State set in the middle of his loyalties to so many other groups. To say that this new conception of the meaning of honesty is wanted is not to deny that there is also need for plain emphasis on the meticulous care one should take of public property. It is notorious that people are slower to damage or to pilfer the property of individuals than that which belongs to large companies or governments. Perhaps we have never been clear enough about what a man does when he steals. The corrective is a slow positive one, and has a great deal to do with bringing back into consciousness the metaphysical connection between men which shows the seriousness of sin with added emphasis. This is obvious, but we perish through neglect of the obvious. The artist delights us by revealing to our dull eyes the significance of the obvious, the theologian has a similar task. His task includes such things as the re-interpretation of honesty right up to the Christian interpretation of being human. This interpretation includes all his lesser tasks, and in so far as it is true will indicate the dangers and the dignity of being human.

There has been a consistent effort to show that a man achieves his dignity through his occupation. Much valuable sociological comment has been made by those who have undertaken this, and all who would study the present social situation owe much to them. However, the fact remains that the bulk of the laity still consider that to live a full Christian life in the community one must be a parson, a doctor, a nurse, a teacher, or possibly an agriculturalist. The bulk of laymen who are serious about religion, at some point consider the possibility of ordination; in many cases lack of education causes them to give up what was little more than a pious aspiration, a notion. Little has been said to help the girl who earns her living by sending out circulars advertising some useless commodity; she might be advised to attend a night-school, though she may well be one of those whose attendance at a night-school would just be attendance. Nor has much advice been given to those who prepare such a girl for confirmation. (One wonders what is said to confirmation candidates about their daily work). Be it right or wrong, in this society there are many occupations which can bring little or no satisfaction to those who follow them and there are many who have not got the intelligence to do anything except a routine job. What can we say? We cannot plead the importance of a job which has no importance as a job. Colonel Blimp might, if it had anything do to with the Export Drive. Canon Blimp is apt to be enthusiastic over someone who is 'doing a real job for the community.' Anyone who thinks about work as a means of achieving human dignity and talks about Occupation as Vocation must be prepared to address parsons, dustmen, miners, chorus girls, nuns, charwomen, soldiers, manicurists, professional golfers, civil servants, helpless invalids, ward maids in hospitals and so on. To say something that might be considered helpful by such a variety of people is, of course, no criterion of truth, but to remember them is a useful discipline in the pursuit of truth, where such pursuit is to be more than ideas about ideas of an idea of the truth.

No occupation satisfies all the needs of a human being. We are not made to be satisfied by the making of things alone. In the Genesis story, it was not work (an occupation) that Adam needed to complete him, but companionship. When a baby is born he at once becomes part of the whole human family; as he grows through boyhood into manhood he becomes, or should become, aware of the complexity of his relationships with other human beings and groups of human beings. These relationships are not single-line relationships, they run through the groups to which he belongs into other groups, and all these groups are inside one inclusive group, however amorphous it may be. The fact that a man belongs to many groups at the same time – family, Trade Union, clubs, societies, parish, church – confuses his thinking and willing, if it does not cause him to cease both. If he is too loyal to one group, he finds himself in the intolerable position of fighting against himself as a member of another group. He cannot decide to belong to no formal groups, or even to limit the number of his memberships by anything more than abandoning clubs and societies of a particular sort. This conflict of loyalties within a man makes his relationships with every other human being more complicated than he knows. To serve many groups makes action seem almost impossible. In passing, note the tensions in any ecclesiastical committee, where every member belongs to at least three other ecclesiastical committees. There is strain in such a committee and a mathematical urge to mark plainly the boundary lines within which each committee's good works are permissible. The committee of a new organisation has the burden of discovering some unoccupied territory, however tiny and vaguely defined it may be. Committee meetings are the prelude to aspirin. It is not without point that the four Gospels say little directly about work, but much about the obligations laid upon men by their relationships to one another.

To everyone born the church can say 'Your vocation is to be human', not human in the abstract; to put it in the clear language of a child – 'Your vocation is to be you. You must be you. You cannot be somebody else.' You do not find yourself by merely reflecting about yourself. You find yourself by

allowing yourself to be aware of the strength of the ties which
bind you to your fellows. As it were, these ties tauten you into
shape, and only then can the shape begin to have its unique
content, provided that none of these ties is resented. If ties are
persistently resented, then there is madness. The shape begins
to have its unique content when obligations are understood
and attempts made to fulfil them. All this the church can say to
a pagan. It also says this to the baptised, but much more as
well. The most significant things a man does are in obedience
to the claims of relationships. These claims begin at birth and
are interpreted through baptism. Baptism does not alter the
consequences of birth, it illuminates them.

It is through relationships that a man reacts towards his full
stature. Work is necessary to him because it is one of the ways
in which he fulfils his obligations to his fellows. It is not that
relationships are incidental to work. This needs to be said
because there is so much talk about the 'importance of pulling
together to get the job done', about team work, about the
importance of personal relationships in the factory if the output
is to be satisfactory. (We have always to be on our guard, the
church is prone to take over the social techniques of the
previous decade into its life – the maze of committees and the
bureaucracy, the influence of democratic ideas, the dizzy effects
of advertising.) It is essential to give the realisation and
maintaining of relationships their proper place, with
occupation as secondary, else we are in the position of implying
that unless a man follows a particular occupation in a particular
type of social order he has no chance of being human or
Christian. The saints could be saints in Ceasar's household.
One wonders what their several occupations were in that
establishment. This is not to say that one does not need to decry
the present social order as evil, on the grounds that the evil of it
does not ultimately matter for those who live under it. Of
course Christians, provided they know what they are doing,
must be active to support social reform or even revolution. But
they are to remember that a new social order will not do away
with all injustices, and some people will still be placed in
occupations which give them little chance of finding dignity in
work. There is a faint liberal hang-over discernible in the hopes
that are contained in some Christian statements, there being an
implication that while it is absurd to work for utopia it is

possible to produce a far better social order . . . and the characteristic 'if only' is added, together with 'we must get . . .'.

To be sure the kind of work a man does has a profound effect upon him, and we could wish that all men had the best possible kind of work to do. But suppose that could be attained, we have still to remember the brevity of all earthly occupations. There will be no carpenters in heaven, but there will be men who have become adult in the fulfilling of the obligations laid upon them through their birth. The manipulation of things, the making of things is not the enduring work of man. The manipulation of words has only point when by it communication of the truth to another person is achieved. The poet, while he may not be widely understood by his contemporaries, is doing the significant in that he is teaching us how to interpret and talk about experience. Art for art's sake is false, so is occupation for occupation's sake, so is the equation of vocation with occupation. The vocation is to be human, and one fulfils that vocation by using whatever gifts one has in answer to the demands of one's fellows, that is, to answer the call of God to be human. No one is so poor that he has no gifts at all. The picture of raising all men up to the standard of B.A., so that they have a chance of following 'The Occupations' is comic if it had not in it such futility, such possibility for disillusionment and discontent, in its materialistic denial of the diversity of gifts.

The Catholic view of life, while far from denying the value of education (if it is education that is under discussion and not something like education), holds that a full human life is possible for all, even the ineducable; that the full human life is possible for those of all occupations, except those which are notoriously sinful. It requires qualities within the reach of all to realise what the implications of birth are for a man, provided that simple people are not confused by those who do not take birth seriously and are far more liberalistic, materialistic and individualistic than they know. The Johannine writings do not adjure us to be careful in our choice of work, rather we are told 'Little children, love one another'; this, as it has been said, we can turn into a platitude or realise that it is the most profound remark that can be addressed to persons, whether they are baptised or not; for the remark is made in the full realisation of the metaphysical results of birth. To hate anyone is to hate self.

This is not to condone any theory of enlightened self-love. If we say God is our Father, the fact of his Fatherhood shows us how fundamental our connection with one another is. The Johannine phrase is an abbreviation of our Lord's Summary of the Law – 'You shall love the Lord your God with all your heart, and with all your soul and with all your mind. This is the great and first commandment. And a second is like to it, You shall love your neighbour as yourself.' Love God, love your neighbour, love yourself. Love can be described as obedience within a relationship. 'Love' says the church, 'is the one activity which can include the whole of a man's life.' To love yourself is to know your deepest needs and strive to satisfy them according to the abilities which are yours. Our deepest needs are concerned with deliverance from the fragmentary life which is ours until baptism uncovers for us the meaning of being human. 'He who loses his life shall find it'. That is, he that ceases to regard himself as a closed entity shall find himself as part of a living whole. 'Theology is only pure when it is applied', Wescott used to say. What are we to tell workers in shops, mines, bakeries, cafés and offices? Are we to imply to them that their life is hopeless on account of the kind of work that they are doing but that someone ought to do something to bring about a new social order, if they will wait? The intelligent will at once ask 'What are we to do while we are waiting?' Academic minds are disturbed by those who want to know what to do. There is need to discover simple words which are capable of expressing a great deal about the enduring work a man does when he lives true to his connectedness with his family, his fellow-workers, employers and friends. Though finally it is not merely a matter of finding words, the right words cannot be found if the assumptions we make about man are false and confused, if theological schizophrenia remains undetected – and it is hard to detect for its causes are psychological not logical. Here we remember the ineptness of much of what is said about being human. How people must be weary of 'must' and 'ought' with seldom a 'why' and rarely a 'how'. For people are puzzled about how they should treat one another, but perhaps parsons are puzzled too. The liberal-individualistic conception of man lingers hiddenly on long after the days of the glory of individual enterprise and that healthy competition which was much for the good of trade.

Work-a-day men and work-a-day women are bewildered through lack of a pattern of conduct in an order of society which is rapidly changing almost in the ways the diagnosers have foretold.

'It is easy to be a saint, if you have not got to bother about being human.' It is impossible to be human if you are not concerned with being a saint (whether you be in Ceasar's household or elsewhere): sainthood is not the obliteration of humanity but its development. This development is at once easy and difficult, such is the nature of grace, such is the nature of man.

DISCIPLESHIP: NOT PEACE BUT A SWORD [1]

'Think not that I am come to send peace on earth; I came not
to send peace but a sword' said the Lord. The sword is sharp to
cut; it stands for selection, severance and struggle. He who
takes the sword shall perish on the Cross, which perishing is
not death but life. The sword stands for struggle; S. Augustine
says 'Be bold in fighting, but without haughtiness.'

'Have I found joy? . . . No, but I
found My joy and that is something
wildly different . . . The Joy of
Jesus can be personal, it can belong
to a single man and he is saved.
He is at peace, he is joyful now
and for always, but he is alone.
The isolation of this joy does
not trouble him; on the contrary
he is the chosen one. In his
blessedness he passes through the
battlefield with a rose in his
hand . . . When I am beset with
affliction, I cannot find peace
in the blandishments of genius.
My joy will not be lasting unless
it is the joy of all. I will not
pass through the battlefield with
a rose in my hand.' [2]

'I will not pass through the battlefield with a rose in my
hand.' Religion that is expressed only in solitude degenerates
into a precious soul-culture. We are not technicians of
individual salvation, showing others a technique for private
use. 'I will not pass through the battlefield with a rose in my
hand.' In a world where there is much unquiet, much cruelty,
much impurity, I must not set out to maintain my own peace,

---

[1] This meditation was first used at the S.C.M. 'Study Swanwick'
conference in July 1953 and published in *The Student Movement* in
December 1954.

[2] *Les vraies richesses*, Jean Giono, quoted by H. de Lubac in *Catholicism*.
English translation published by Burns Oates, 1950.

my own gentleness of heart, and my own purity at any cost. He that preserves his own things for his own use, loses them, destroying much through this irresponsibility. I cannot walk the quiet corridors of my own mind and find the peace of God in a shrine deeply secluded within my own being unless I am also active in the vulgarity, the hideousness and the beauty of day-to-day living with its savagery and its gentleness entwined, with truth and falsehood strangely mixed, where just men often act unjustly and unjust men minister justice in the name of a society that both assents to and dissents from the principles upon which justice is based.

How we sigh for a straight fight, with the sides neatly drawn up, wearing discernible uniforms and crying distinctive battle-cries. Instead the air is full of darkness and dust and rolled garments, one shouting one thing and another another thing, allies continually changing sides without awareness of the change. We could bear to give up the intolerable struggle with words and meanings, we could bear to give up the endless risks of significant action in a situation we only partly understand . . . 'How often would I wash my hands of the whole sorry business, but that strange Man on the Cross keeps calling me back' [3] The peace he offers is cold and sharp, cold as steel and sharp as steel, but it is an assurance that the struggle is not in vain. We are not those who beat the air.

We are not technicians of individual salvation. The worship and service of God can only be authentic when a pattern of movements made in solitude and in society is being woven. Fundamentally the Gospel is obsessed with the idea of the unity of human society. It is not for merely moral reasons and moral results that Christians care for society. When Peter Claver went down into the stench of the galleys and stooped to dress the festering wounds made by the rubbing of rusty chains, he spoke with infinite gentleness to each of the slaves and he was talking to them about their sins. Whatever the circumstances, a man is responsible before God for his reaction to those circumstances; we both make and are made by our circumstances. We are not puppets, we are not parasites, we are persons; 'there's a divinity that shapes our ends, rough hew them how we will.' This shaping is not an automatic

[3] Fr. Tyrell to von Hügel.

force; it is the power of the Word made flesh, the Word that was before ever the earth and the world were made. The Word, spoken, calls us to participate in his ceaseless creative activity.

Profound living is not the enjoyment of the fragrance of a rose carried delicately through the battlefield. To live profoundly, creatively, includes awareness of the carnage in a sincerity that is without sanctimoniousness or sentimentality; in a sincerity that does not mistake fastidiousness for virtue just as it does not mistake for sanctity a desire to keep one's hands clean at all costs. We remember the reek of cigarettes and beer, the chromium and the noise; the shadowy figures in doorways, the tentative greetings, the light in greedy eyes. We remember the sad-faced man who has missed every modest goal he set himself and the woman who knows that she has neither charm nor brains. We remember the loud hysterical laugh in which there is no mirth but just a brief relief from nerves too taut. We are not technicians of individual salvation, but many of our works of mercy consist in tending those who have battered and bruised themselves in some skirmish on the fringe of life or at its very centre. 'I will not pass through the battlefield with a rose in my hand.'

Out of that strife, this peace;
At pain's far point there grows,
Beyond the stabbing thorns,
This dark, dark rose. [4]

By an old symbolism, the five petals of the rose stand for the five wounds of Christ, its fragrance standing for the unutterable benefits of His Passion. The benefits of His Passion cannot be a private possession . . . 'My joy will not be lasting unless it is the joy of all . . . I will not pass through the battlefield with a rose in my hand.'

[4] From a poem by Muriel Grainger, published in the magazine of the English Association.

THE LOVE OF GOD REFLECTED IN US

And all shall be well and
All manner of thing shall be well
By the purification of the motive
In the ground of our beseeching.

                              T. S. Eliot – Little Gidding III

The purification is not wish without grace,
Nor is it grace without wish,
Nor is it wish and grace without deed
Any more than it is deed without wish and grace.

The way of purification is the way of obedience,
Obedience is response to the drawing of the love of God,
Obedience is the answer to the voice of his calling.

God concentrates the drawing of this love and this calling
Into a fine point whenever the bread is broken
And the wine poured out; then we see as we often see
That the wonder of all he makes hides
The single vast wonder that is himself.

Every increase in our knowledge of God is a demand for
further obedience to him. He does not compel obedience; the
urgency of the demand is generated by love, and love is not
marked by our passivity but by active response to him in whom
all love begins, in whom all power has its source. Love is not
the abandonment of power, love is the use of power; love is not
the destruction of self, love is the affirmation of self. Love is
concerned with neither obliteration nor deformation; love is
concerned with transformation, with affirmation. Love never
can be described as renunciation; renunciation is only justifiable
when it is part of the movement of affirmation, but there must
be renunciation; we must select and reject or there can be no
significant expression of love, and therefore no love. It is the
affirmation which makes renunciation inevitable and
meaningful; renunciation is never a good thing in itself. We
never deny ourselves just for the sake of denying ourselves, we
deny ourselves that we may take up the cross and follow him
and be his disciple. If we are to follow him we cannot follow

him in a way of our own devising, we can only follow him by
hearing his voice and paying heed to it:

> . . . And you shall love the Lord your
> God with all your heart, and with all
> your soul, and with all your mind,
> and with all your strength. The
> second is like, You shall love your
> neighbour as yourself.

MARK 12 30-31

The commandment is threefold: Love God, love your
neighbour, love yourself. To love myself is to control myself.
How can I love my neighbour unless I am able to curb my
impatience and my impetuosity? Love is clear-sighted, how can
I love my neighbour and work to give him what he needs if I do
not know what I need myself? How can I understand the
content of any man's plight if I have not lived enough and
loved enough to know the power of manifold temptations?
How can I put up with others if I cannot put up with myself?
People who do not care for themselves are touchy; they see
slights and insults where they were neither planned nor
intended; they expect their neighbours to have as bad an
opinion of them as they have of themselves. A man who does
not care for himself can care for no one and no one can care for
him without difficulties which often prove too great for natural
man.

Some do not care for themselves because they cannot forgive
themselves. A cannot forgive himself because he is not
charming, popular and clever. B can never forgive himself
because he knows that he will always be a rather dull third-rate
scholar. C can never forgive herself because she is not lovely,
witty and successful, treading soft carpets and important
platforms with equal poise. D can never forgive himself for a
lost opportunity seven and a half years ago. E can never forgive
himself because he is far from holy. F covers up his despair
about himself with a perpetual series of jokes about his
shortcomings, or else with too many and too frank exposures of
his weaknesses in an attempt to acquire honesty and humility
which can only be got in one way, for honesty and humility are
given, not struggled after and possessed. No man can forgive

himself, no man can deal with his own guilt. No man can apologise to himself for failing to be what he longs to be – how can a man split himself in two? How could be he sure that the apology was genuine? How could he know he had accepted his own apology? No man can forgive his neighbour's sin or justify his neighbour – such things are not lightly given and lightly received. Forgiveness and justification are in God who is all in all. Forgiveness and justification are only possible within the living sphere which God has brought into being, that is, within the common life of the Body of Christ. Life in that sphere is not restricted, for this is the sphere where temporal and eternal interpenetrate. In this sphere there are no boundary walls; there is only the horizon's rim and the limitless distances beyond. The common life of the Body of Christ takes us everywhere, for the realms of obedience are vast.

Sometimes in the name of safety and self-love a man tries to restrict the movements of his life within an area of his own choosing; such a life becomes stifling and intolerable. An intelligent man soon sees the self-made limitations looming round him, closing him in and bringing him to the treadmill of a little round of thoughts; on this treadmill the steps of every argument are well worn, the memories of all that has been not to be again are like the fading photographs in the old and well-thumbed album – even daydreams become stale and brief. No one can live for very long on safety and on the past. The safety becomes tiresome and the past a mockery. If a man in the name of safety and self-love sets out to manage and control his own life by his own power, he loses all power to control or manage. *'Entre les mains de Dieu, je suis mon maître'*. Between the hands of God I am master of myself. I cannot abide myself unless I abide in God. I cannot love myself unless I love God. God requires me to love myself. Thou shalt love thy neighbour as thyself. You are to love your neighbour the way you love yourself. In doing this, what the world means by danger is safety, and what the world means by safety is danger. In the world a man clutches at his identity, is intent on preserving his importance and proclaiming his value as a person. Like happiness, identity and importance and value are only found and preserved when they are forgotten in pursuit of something else.

We love ourselves by making the best use of ourselves and the best use of ourselves is to do the highest thing we can with

ourselves: 'and here we offer and present unto thee, O Lord,
ourselves, our souls and bodies . . .' But how do we make the
offering? Not in a way of our own choosing but in the way of
his choosing, by giving ourselves up entirely to do his will in
each circumstance of life, in the sanctuary, in the study, in
solitude, in society, in the pulpit. His will is to be found in the
acts that love enlightens and which enliven our consciousness.
To love him is to rejoice in this extension of our awareness and
to act in accordance with this widened awareness. Every act of
obedience to what St. Paul would teach us to call the heavenly
vision leads us further and further into the darkness which is
the light of God. In this darkness we perform deeds we do not
fully understand, yet they are neither the fruits of whims nor of
folly. We are not being irrational, we are like the artist who
knows he is painting something too big for words or like the
scientist who knows that he is about to discover something
beyond the reach of common knowledge. God is always
prompting us to leave the familiar, or rather to use the familiar
as a pathway out into the unknown.

Let us turn our minds again to him who not only gives us
sufficient certainty for faith but who is also concerned to lead us
into the fullness of life, who is concerned to help us to make the
most positive affirmation of ourselves. 'On the same night that
he was betrayed, he took bread . . .' We see him surrounded by
his disciples. The lamp burns brightly throwing shadows in the
corners of the room. Cups, plates, scraps of bread and scattered
crumbs on the table show that supper is over; there is the dish
from which Judas received the sop, there is the door that Judas
shut so recently, the remaining disciples have forgotten about
him. There is the sound of the familiar voice saying unfamiliar
things . . .

A new commandment I give to you, that
you love one another; even as I have
loved you, that you also love one another.
By this all men will know that you
are my disciples, if you have love
for one another.

JOHN 13 34-35

We offer ourselves to him by loving one another the way he loves us. We can describe his love for us by the helpless cry of a newly born babe, by the closing of the carpenter's shop, by his baptism. We can go on to describe his love by considering the bleakness and the sharpness of the Mount of Temptation, the angry faces in synagogues and in the Court of the Gentiles. We can go on to describe his love for us by considering the disarranged cups and plates and the crumbs which showed that a meal had ended, we can look at the torchlight in the Garden, the firelight in the courtyard, we can listen to the roar of the mob and the fear alternating with anger in Pilate's voice. We can listen to some of the words spoken on the Via Dolorosa and at the place called Golgotha, the Place of a Skull: 'Weep not for me but weep for yourselves and for your children . . .', 'If thou be the Son of God, come down from the Cross . . .' We can look at the open tomb in the dawn of the new day. The signs are familiar to us; we try to pierce through them again and again in an attempt to see more fully the love which they express. His love is not himself; in his mercy he vouchsafes to us glimpses of his being in those fleeting moments when we are aware that all things are ours because they are his and because his is ours and we are his. Love of him without clamour and insistence brings awareness of ourselves in him and of him in us. We could never deserve such a matchless thing. We cannot, we dare not demand by right what we are given in love. In love we find that demand, rights, rewards, merits are conceptions which belong to something less than the love wherewith we are loved and with which we would love. Having said that, we remember that love is expressed both in truth and in justice.

In love of him without clamour and insistence we gradually begin to see more and more clearly what happened between the time of the cock crowing, the shouts of the crowd, the banging of the hammer and the commotion in the garden at dawn. In love of him we see a little more clearly what is happening through all that he is doing now. The altar is the focal point. What he creates, and nothing exists outside him, he creates for all. The altar not only speaks of creation, it speaks of the completion of creation in redemption. The unconsecrated bread on the altar is eloquent of man's participation in the unceasing creative work of God. The consecrated bread which is given and received speaks of man's active part in the work of redemption. Let me use the words of another: "The redemption then must be realized in us. A mere 'application', while we remain in a purely passive attitude, is altogether insufficient . . . it is a living and active part which we take in the redemptive work of Christ, a part which will be passive, certainly, in that Christ acts in us but also really active in that we are associated with this work by an action . . . How is it possible to realize a work of such sublimity? . . . The answer is given by our Lord, who has instituted for us the mysteries of the Liturgy, that is, the sacred actions which we perform but which our Lord (by the ministry of the church's priests) realizes simultaneously in us. By these actions we can participate in the redemptive acts of Christ . . . The mystery of Christ, which was accomplished in our Lord in all its historical and physical reality, is realized in us in symbol, beneath representative and figurative forms. Yet these are not mere appearances . . . they communicate to us the full reality of the new life which Christ our Mediator offers to us. This altogether special sort of participation in Christ's life, which is both presented beneath the expression of a symbol and at the same time really effected was called by the first Christians 'mystic participation'." [1]

In creation and in redemption we have our active part signified by the unconsecrated bread and by the consecrated bread. Neither creation nor redemption, neither the unconsecrated bread nor the consecrated bread can be considered without reflecting that God makes to give and gives that we may make. The gifts of God are never so huge that they leave our effort superfluous nor are they so meagre as to make our activity impossible. He gives ceaselessly and freely only on one condition, that is, that we receive what he gives. To receive what he gives means freeing our hands from wrong occupations and freeing our minds from the storm and fury of wrong desires and false hopes; it means giving up and throwing away all that the world teaches us to care about in order that we may receive all he teaches us to care about. This receiving is the act of love, a threefold act of love – love of self, love of neighbour, love of God. In our life with God, what we

---

[1] Dom Odo Casel, quoted in *Christ in the Liturgy*, Dom Illtyd Trethowan, p.16.

receive from him is the beginning of everything we do and are.
Receptivity is the highest act; in it there is the double
movement of abandoning and attending, abandoning what
the world teaches us to care for that we may attend to God. If
we do not deliberately pay attention to him, the attention we
deliberately give to his creatures is more loss than gain. We can
be so interested in the properties of bread that we neglect him
who makes it and makes us capable of investigation and
observation. We can be so interested in the proper ceremonies
concerning the consecrated bread that we neglect him who
took our flesh upon him that he might free us from the
bondage of trivialities and bring us into the width and depth of
his glory. All good things are both powerful and dangerous;
naturally the greater the things the more powerful and the
more dangerous they are. Fear of danger can prevent the
mature worship and service of God. 'When I became a man',
said St. Paul, 'I put away childish things'. It is childish to
welcome danger because it means adventure; it is childish to
shrink from accepting the fact that danger is inevitable in life.
There can be no avoidance of danger, physical and spiritual, for
either the children of darkness or the children of light. We
cannot make ourselves safe, there are no precautions we can
take. Our safety is in God, who knows our tasks and our
dangers, who will not destroy us either by pampering us or
neglecting us. He does not make the threats of the Valley of the
Shadow of Death innocuous. This world is full of the threat of
death, death physical and death spiritual. Priest and people
alike know the dangers; they also know the strength of God
when they have become accustomed to the manifestations of
Perfect Strength in all their difference from the pretentious
displays of strength by which the lesser powers of darkness
show themselves. We cannot make ourselves safe, but we can
be safe in God in whom we live and move and have our being.
He will always receive us so long as we are ready to receive
him. Therefore receptivity is the highest activity. Receptivity is
not only expectancy and attention; it is also taking and keeping
what is given – love, joy, peace, long-suffering, gentleness,
goodness, faith, meekness, temperance. We find the reality of
the gift and the reality of our possession of it not by analysis but
by use, and the use is not a solitary occupation. Thou shalt love
the Lord thy God, Thou shalt love thy neighbour as thyself.

We can only find ourselves in God, but he has made us so that we can only find him through things and through one another . . . 'this is the Way, walk ye in it'. The Lord is not only the road but he is the journey's end as well; the road, the walking and the end are all one in him who is the source of our life and the ground of our beseeching.

As we kneel at the altar, the bread of life is broken and given to the pilgrims, and we know what it is to be neither at home in this world, nor in the other world; we also know, if even a little, how he reconciles us to our present unrest not only by the foretaste of the final rest in him but by the assurance that our oblation of ourselves to him now is our participation in the unchanging. The sand may move, slide from under our feet, but below the sand there is the Rock.

> Suffer us not to mock ourselves with
> falsehood
> Teach us to care and not to care
> Teach us to sit still
> Our peace in his will.
>   T. S. Eliot – Ash Wednesday

> And all shall be well and
> All manner of thing shall be well
> By the purification of the motive
> In the ground of our beseeching.
>   T. S. Eliot – Little Gidding III

LOVING AND BEING LOVABLE

He came to his own home and his
own people received him not . . .

JOHN 1 ¹¹

'Teacher, which is the great
commandment in the law?'

MATTHEW 22 ³⁶

Some time during the last few days of our Lord's earthly
ministry this question was asked. It is easy to picture the crowd
pressing close to him in the Court of the Gentiles, a crowd
made up of the friendly, the curious and the hostile. On the
fringe of this crowd people moved without even a glance in his
direction. The Pharisees after hearing of the failure of the
Sadducees' question gathered themselves together and made a
further attempt to trap him. St. Matthew describes the incident
in these sentences ". . . One of them, a lawyer, asked him a
question, to test him, 'Teacher, which is the great
commandment in the law?' And he said to him, 'You shall love
the Lord your God with all your heart, and with all your soul
and with all your mind. This is the great and first
commandment. And a second is like it, You shall love your
neighbour as yourself. On these two commandments depend
all the law and the prophets'." Doctrinally his answer was
incontestable. In effect he said that the three-fold injunction to
love both presupposed and expressed all that was revealed by
God through the law and the prophets. His answer is an echo
of the Sermon on the Mount: 'Think not that I am come to
destroy the law or the prophets. I am not come to destroy, but
to fulfil.' That is, he came to supply what was lacking in the
law and the prophets. His enemies saw the law and the
prophets as indispensable and sufficient in themselves as a
guide to living. He could not have it that a code and exposition
of a code would be enough guidance for human behaviour in
ever-changing and ever unique human situations. On being
questioned about the great commandment he made the
orthodox reply. Both he and his questioners meant different
things by the same words.

Christians in this age, as in every age, have to see the

implications of this threefold injunction to love. We know that if
we love the Word we shall also love the world and that if we
love the world we will love the Word. The Word was before the
world, without him nothing is made that is made; he even
makes the very light by which we see him. In looking for him
we do not strain our eyes to see his dramatic entrance into the
life of the world. We look for him in the world in things and
happenings; we look for him in the lives of men for we expect
to see him most characteristically in the highest form of his
creation which we know. When we thus look for him in things,
happenings and people we find that we are in touch with the
movements of life which are in the very depth of our own
being. So it is, love begins in faith; faith in the existence of God,
faith in his ceaseless creative activity, faith in ourselves as men,
faith in the reality of our powers of mind and soul. There could
be no looking for God if we thought there was nothing to see;
there would be no looking if we did not believe in our ability to
perceive and know. When we affirm the Christian faith we
affirm belief both in God and in man. Therefore when we love
and talk about loving God, neighbours and ourselves, we are
making profound doctrinal statements. What do men need and
what can men give one another, is a question which buddhist,
communist, hindu, atheist, agnostic and Christian would
answer in different ways. That is to say, 'love' is a word which
becomes the starting point of the differences between
Christianity and non-Christianity. Love demands that we know
what we can give to others and how we give it and this
knowledge can only be derived from our belief in ourselves and
in our connection with one another. That belief rests on the fact
that when our Lord told us to love one another he was telling
us to do something that could be done. He did not set out to tell
us what exactly to do on specific occasions but rather he
described a habitual disposition to be maintained by those who
would love and be loved.

Christianity shows us that our love for others is not entirely
dealt with when one talks of the Gospel works of mercy, caring
for the sick and needy, the captives and the forlorn. These are
obvious indications to specific acts of love but we also have to
love the strong, the merry, those holier than we are; all who
succeed in art, literature, science, politics – and it is difficult to
express love for the strong and the successful in life,

particularly when it is the sort of success we approve. This love calls for generous acts of appreciation and enjoyment of the achievements of others as well as a readiness to console the sorrowful and oppressed. Perhaps it is most difficult of all to keep on being interested in and agreeable to those men and women who, in our estimation, live humdrum fortellable lives. That sometimes is more testing than the continued love of the callous, the hard and cruel, the open enemies who can, in our bad moments, give us material both for excited sensation and self-righteous indignation.

We say that a man is faithful considering him from one aspect. Thinking of him from the aspect of Christian love we hesitate to say a man is lovable on account of the rather odd way that the term 'lovable' is used, but it could be used to indicate the man who does not tempt people by general disagreeableness, small-mindedness. There is a sense in which it is true to say that it is sinful to be unlovable. Unlovableness provokes others to sin, whether by making favourable comparisons, or by open aggression or the hidden aggression of wanting to have a good influence at all costs. To be lovable is not merely to have endearing ways or to be a public figure with an enthusiastic following. A lovable person never gives the impression that he has gone to a lot of trouble to do what he has done for you. On the other hand when he is the recipient he generously accepts help from others; he does not resent the fact that someone is in a position to do something for him which he cannot do for himself, and he does not draw attention to the fact that you have put yourself out to help him. Most people, perhaps unconsciously, are disturbed by those whose lavish gratitude shows surprise that anyone should go to any trouble for others, and the phrase 'specially for me', if used, gives the impression that the speaker thinks himself alone capable of giving rise to such an unusual display of generosity – all small points perhaps, too much splitting of hairs about unimportant trifles in everyday behaviour, but it is in the unimportant acts that a man makes himself and others. It is by a multiplicity of small acts that he expresses his hope that others will fulfil their vocation to be human; but the magic is not just in the acts: there is a communication of power from one person to others when the acts truly belong to the man in the sense of being typical of him.

You shall love the Lord your God . . . you shall love your neighbour as yourself. How can I love my neighbour as myself if he will not allow me? There is risk in love: much damage can be done, and often is done, but there is a distinction to be made between damage done in affection and the damage done by the one who stops at nothing to ensure his own safety, moral, spiritual or physical. Lovableness does not automatically call out a loving response. In the Court of the Gentiles the lawyer came with others who could be called as witnesses; he asked his question clearly and politely. The answer was given; you can almost see the lawyer lifting one shoulder in a gesture of hopelessness or perhaps he made no outward sign of his failure to trap the one whose love made him a public enemy.

How is one to love and be lovable? We know the answer even if we have not the words for it. We make it by thinking of the broken bread on the supper table, the rough wood of the cross and the tomb broken open. How is one to love and be lovable? We do not deserve to have such capabilities; God gives them to us but we are to take them. Through taking the broken bread we become hard enough to pick up the rough wood and strong enough to break open the tomb.

THE CITY

A modern city with its tall buildings, its wonderful use of glass, its swift moving traffic, its shop windows displaying such a wide variety of things, its neon lights, all combine to make it a symbol as well as an actual expression of human power to take things and use them to make an entity as physically complex as a city. A modern city speaks of other human achievements by its churches, universities, schools, hospitals, blocks of offices, electric coolers and gasometers. In among these buildings narrow dark streets twist their way into other narrow dark streets, and here are houses too small and cramped for family dwellings; here are the brothels, the seedy pubs, the doss-houses and all the other things which comfortable citizens like to forget. The blemishes which mar every human achievement do not cancel the greatness of human achievements. No one would expect sinlessness in a city any more than he would look for sanctity in every rural area.

A city only has importance as a place on account of the people who live in it. It is a considerable human achievement for people to live in such constant proximity to one another without destroying one another. It is an extraordinary thing that urban man has such control over himself and that communal life is as orderly as it is. The queue, the regular supply of milk and bread, the postal service, the public transport systems are maintained for reasons other than that people are doing the work they are paid for.

It was comparatively easy to live in a rural community, specially a century ago, because a good deal of work was done single-handed (for example, the stone-breaker, the farm labourer thinning turnips or herding cattle) and neighbours busy and distant. The bustle of a market day with its medley of frightened ungovernable animals was never as disturbing as city streets on any shopping day of the week. The greater the community in size the more a tax is made on the individual both from the point of view of the restraint he must exercise over his passions and the difficulty of continuing to believe in his significance as an individual. We have every right to say that the city is a training ground for human greatness. The building of cities is an expression of that greatness and there is further the fact that human beings live in reasonable order and in sufficient peace to provide the conditions which stimulate the development of scientists, philosophers, poets, painters, legislators, musicians, saints, and a host of others who live useful, even beautiful, but unlabellable lives.

Human life can only be fully lived where both great evil and great goodness are possible. In our world a city fulfils this condition. To make use of a rabbinical saying: God does not live in a city but he works there just as he does not live in the countryside but works there. There was a notion that one could be nearer to God in the unspoiled country (that is, untouched by man) than in a man-made city. There is still in a great many of us an unconscious or unexamined feeling that God made the countryside and man the city. But in fact man did much in the shaping of the country as we have known it. Men felled trees, cleared forests, drained swamps, dug harbours out of rocks, ploughed the land, dug canals and changed the course of rivers. But man cannot work without God; without him is not anything made that is made whether it be a small garden or a gasometer. We all agree in the wonder of God's direct creation – the width of the sky, the distance of stars, the vivid beauty of the rainbow and the changing colour of the mountains. But is it less wonderful for God to make a mountain than to make beings capable of building cities and ordering and living in metropolitan communities?

The highest work of man is in the city; the city is the most characteristic human work in the whole of creation; it is the most intense sphere of human living. In it we know ourselves as men through our several occupations and abilities; we find ourselves in one another, and in this process we are also discovering, whether we know it or not, that we are finding God in ourselves and ourselves in God and God in our neighbours and our neighbours in him.

Let us look again at the solitary figure in the middle of the cheering crowd approaching the gates of the city on the first Palm Sunday. When he beheld the city he wept. He had no illusions about the city, he knew he would be rejected yet he did not even pause at its gates. Love sheds all illusions, even the final illusion of thinking one has no illusion left. Love sheds illusions in order to love men and women as they are and not as love would like to find them. In his humanity our Lord knew the human tendency to live on illusions when the bitterness of reality makes love too painful.

BEYOND THE CITY

He came to his own home . . .   JOHN 1 11

Unless the Lord builds the house,
Those who build it labour in vain.
Unless the Lord watches over the city,
The watchman stays awake in vain.

PSALM 127 1

He without whom the city could not have been built wept
when he came to its gates knowing that the day would come
when there would be neither gates nor walls nor city left. Not
many years later the uneasy national tension snapped and the
calculated fury of the Roman professional legions scattered the
ill-equipped untrained patriots and Jerusalem was left no more
than heaps of burning rubble.

Unless the Lord watches over the city
The watchman stays awake in vain.

He would not save the city in spite of its inhabitants because
he has shown that there are things more valuable than the
safety of the city and its inhabitants. These things have been
manifested by his complete disregard for his own safety; he
kept all these things through the action that seemed the loss of
everything. The crowd stood gaping at him and the high
priests and scribes mocked him: 'Come down from the cross,
come down and we will see and believe'. Everyone within
earshot laughed whether they knew why they were laughing
or not.

Cities do not last forever but in their brief life eternal things
are laid hold on as the Anglican indicates in his petition that we
may so pass through things temporal, that we finally lose not
the things eternal. For the city is one of man's temporal
experiences or rather it is the dynamic setting and centre of his
life in time. Like all temporal acts – such as a work of art, the
literal giving of one's life for another, the unconscious self-
effacement of the humble, the generous gift that escapes even
the appearance of patronage – a city does not remain a visible
separate entity indefinitely. Like all human acts, corporate or

individual, a city has both its beginning and its end in God who also sustains it during the span from its beginning till its ending. What happens during its life is fully understood by God though ungodly city-dwellers have ungodly views of its importance; and the devout, by their devoutness, do not escape the temptation inherent in all human activities, to care more for the temporal things than the eternal. Often the words men use in a city to speak of the great human themes outlast the structure of the city. Stones seem more durable than songs but songs often can last longer.

God is never absent from any city; a city lives and moves and has its being in God. Men cannot banish him but they hasten the city's ending in an attempt to control what is beyond human control. The Babel story puts this truth in story form and history has echoed it in the life and death of city after city, but with death comes resurrection. That is, death does not lay corrupting hands on the things eternal brought to light by men working in and through God who shares all things with us men. Some of us who profess Christian faith and practise it in selected areas of life are practical atheists in other spheres of life as we strive to make ourselves important and secure. Wherever there is this striving after importance and safety, whether individual or collective, the importance achieved is a caricature, and concentration and efficiency in working for safety produces a condition in which men perish spiritually because safety is not enough to live for and within. This we know and the four Gospels tell us we are to love ourselves, our neighbours and God; at the same time they tell us that the things, however good, which we want too intensively we shall not be given, whether we want them for ourselves or to have under our control to give to others. 'The first shall be last and the last first.' 'He that humbleth himself shall be exalted.' (But what happens to the man who humbles himself in order to be exalted?) 'He that findeth his life shall lose it and he that loseth his life for my sake shall find it.' Having lost themselves for the Lord's sake Christians hope that they will recognise themselves as the new beings they find in him.

Unless the Lord watches over the city
The watchman stays awake in vain.

These words are from one of the songs of ascent which pilgrims sang on their way to keep the Feasts in Jerusalem. On the first Palm Sunday they sang this just at the time when the Council of the Jews had come to a conclusion about the steps which must be taken to preserve the safety of the city; they thought of their own and the city's safety bound up in one. Their conclusion was clear; they purposed to destroy the one person who could preserve the safety of the city. His conception of safety was not theirs – his death was, for them, the means of keeping their safety: for him it was the only way to keep his. When men and women are obsessed with the need for an understandable and immediate safety, they may get it for a time but they dwindle in spirit: no one can be forever content with nothing but the maintenance of defences as one's chief concern. Our Lord loved the city but he loved other things better. We are to love our city and we are to love other things more. He always shows us that you cannot fully love a family or a country, your church, unless you love something greater than any of them. The love of family is right and can be beautiful but becomes comic when it is loved better than any other institution so that family birthdays and anniversaries make a calendar parallel to the church calendar. At the same time no one is more false than he who is too holy to accept his proper share of family responsibilities and work. (The whole of St. Matthew 10 is a useful meditation on this subject.) Discipleship calls a man away from the hearth; he may not return to it or he may return with a new understanding of family relationships which may cause a household to be divided through his attitude and his habit of not putting family duties before all others. It is good to talk and think about this strange advice our Lord gives to all who would be safe in him; but happy are we whenever we act according to this advice.

We remember the Jewish council's concern for the peace of Jerusalem and our Lord's grief because he saw the inevitability of its destruction. In modern cities many of us can see possibilities of peace and destruction. Apart from the constant (if mostly unconscious) fear of war, a war of swift immediate wholesale destruction, we wonder whether a city can continue to maintain the cost, in money and personnel, of highly complicated administration. For instance, to provide and distribute electricity, gas, coal for two million people requires highly skilful organisation according to a carefully drawn up system of supply; and men who devise a system to benefit others tend, ultimately, to be more concerned with the improvement and maintenance of the system than with the people they wish to benefit. They are not to be blamed, we are always initiating an activity that takes on a life of its own which is outside our control. This happens in both church and city: we are all in danger of becoming slaves to the systems we draw up and work. In these days we need to reflect constantly on an adaptation of a phrase of our Lord's namely, systems were made for men and not men for systems. We need to resist the multiplication of systems and institutions. Any society, or institution, which is too efficient destroys the creativity of the institution and of the whole society. This observation can be made on both sociological and theological grounds: in saying this, it must be added that theologians have learned a great deal from sociologists, and not least the criteria by which one sees the difference between collectivism and corporateness. Collectivism seizes on what is common to all at the expense of the individual's importance, while corporate life recognises the necessity for a commumity which gives the maximum liberty to each individual without promoting anarchy, not that this liberty can be measured and handed out. No one can give another liberty, each one must take it for himself and although one does not take liberty from others we may feel that we are doing so and others may feel that we are pirates. We take liberty by acting. A man cannot be given the freedom to say what he must say, it remains with him to say it. The anglican collect puts this well when it speaks of the service of God as being perfect freedom. We do not get liberty by performing a special action; we get it in doing the things we ought to and can do. The modern city tends to narrow the areas of life in which significant and free human actions may be practised. Perhaps the special calling of Christians is an acceptance of the limited scope for overt activity of the specifically and conventionally religious sort. This is no more than a particular recognition that the Christian church is not totalitarian but lives through its members, in every city activity. We do not set out to conquer the city in the name of Christ, in a conquest like his our submission must also be like his. God is in the city; we Christians are not to demand from him the right to control all men and manage all human affairs. Power of that order is not ours, but just as a poor man may be obsessed with a desire for money so those called to serve may be obsessed with a desire to dominate.

CHURCH LIFE AND WORKADAY LIFE

He came to his own home and his own
people received him not.

JOHN 1 11

And Jesus entered the temple of God,
and drove out all who sold and bought
in the temple, and he overturned the
tables of the money-changers, and the
seats of those who sold the pigeons.
He said to them, "It is written, 'My
house shall be called a house of prayer':
but you make it a den of robbers."

MATTHEW 21 12-13

The tables of the money-changers and the seats of them that
sold doves were in the shadow of the most sacred building in
the world. Beside the Holy of Holies there was trading,
dishonest trading and fraudulent changing of money into the
required currency. Protest was made from time to time but the
practice continued. Picture the medley of different coloured
clothes, the crowd becoming still and silent – a tense moment
and all eyes fixed on the figure of our Lord with a scourge in his
hands; there is a crash as the tables are flung over, traders and
money-changers shrink back, coins lie scattered on the
ground. Our Lord was blunt: "It is written, 'My house shall be
called a house of prayer': but you make it a den or robbers."
When he said that he was, in effect, talking to the Temple
authorities and, more immediately painful, he was also, in
effect, talking to the people who stood by approving of his
action. The ordinary people hated this abuse of the Temple but
by their inactivity allowed it to go on.

Our Lord did not overthrow the altar, he overthrew the
tables of traders and money-changers. He did not overthrow
the altar because simple devout people in the grace of God
preserved the sanctity of the altar by their prayers. Scores of
priests year by year came to minister in the Temple on their turn
of residence. Their activities are not to be confused with the
powerful political role played by the High Priests who were
always of the Sadducees. The Temple services went on, good

things in themselves; the officiants were good men in their sphere; we would consider that they lived out of society, banishing out of mind all that lay behind our Lord's alarming action when he took the scourge into his hands to make his protest at secularism as practised by Temple authorities and dishonest dealers. It is said the the Temple authorities either rented out space to money-changers and traders or claimed a percentage of the takings. But the authenticity of worship at the altar could not cancel out the badness of dishonesty under the permission of the same authorities as those who maintained the ordering of Temple worship.

Our Lord, described as the friend of publicans and sinners, was shocked by more than the dishonesty he found in the Court of the Gentiles. He was shocked because the one place allowed for Gentiles to pray in the Temple was the open court called the Court of the Gentiles. How could people even safeguard the mood in which prayer might be made in a place like a market?

Our Lord does not overthrow our altars. He overthrows all that is trivial, banal, false and blasphemous which gather at a distance from the altar. The things about the church which non-Christians first see are those things which are at a distance from the altar. Perhaps we can feel grateful that there are no open scandals like those of the Court of the Gentiles but scandals there are. More common and serious is the heap of trivialities which, to use a New Testament phrase, are a bushel that hides the light that is meant to shine before men. Churchmen, like all men, tend to talk a great deal about the weather, modern transport, holidays, traffic jams and so on. Like most men, churchmen tend to avoid serious conversation. One does not mean that churchmen and women are to be for ever preaching to friends and neighbours but rather to be ready to help others to fulfil their vocation to be human, and that is done by men who are intent on fulfilling their own vocation to be human. This often calls for a patience and affection which enables one to listen while another enjoys himself expanding on the excitements and hardships of his occupation and about the things he finds in music or painting. Most of the people we meet are a long way from the altar or even from the steps that lead from the footpath to the west door. The churchman's first concern is not to 'get people to church' but to help them to be human which in some cases will be no more than encouraging criticism of the smallest things like television programmes, first division football, professional boxing and so on. We live in an age in which there is much sophisticated scepticism and much mass-mindedness manufactured through the powers of suggestion at the disposal of modern advertising, television, cinema, the glossy weeklies. It is always difficult in this world to achieve mature adulthood: we need one another, and the churchman is concerned to be what he gives and to give what he is. We would be on fire with life divine so that others may be warmed and illuminated. This can only happen when we have forgotten ourselves, our desire to help as well as our anxieties, our strength and our weakness. This 'forgetfulness' is a ragged way of describing one of the elements of faithfulness. It is best known when experienced in a live person who releases you from all inhibitions because he loves you, himself, the world and God with no conscious intention as to what he wishes to achieve through this love. Love which is too deliberate, too heavy-handed, too purposeful, is an activity which needs another name. Love is restrained and diffident in its expression out of respect for each human person as a being made in the image of God, the highest creative work of God's that is known to us. Love implies the refusal to enforce one's will on another even for the other's good without ever losing one's sense of unity with the other in God through whom this seemingly impossible sort of love becomes practicable and is finally seen not as a virtue but as a necessity.

Our Lord does not overthrow our altars; he turns his attention to the practices which we allow to flourish under their shadow. Things like amusements that no longer amuse, sociabilities that are only sociabilities, much talking, the maintenance of organisations which were essential twenty, thirty and forty years ago but are now no longer needed. There is no point in negative tabulation; he overthrows all things which make worship difficult or a mockery; he overthrows such things as are not relevant in the church's mission in the world now. He does not advance to those of our committee tables, public meetings and organisations which are obscurantist and now obscure of purpose; he does not advance; he makes no flourish with a scourge; he has his agents. Some of his lesser agents make their protest by

resignations or by absences. They are inarticulate, not coherent
in their own minds, but they are bored and embarrassed
because serious people are puzzled by so much of the church's
weekday activities. The more articulate of his agents point the
finger and proclaim and sometimes are understood and
heeded. The church cannot draw up a list of the activities
proper for her members for all of the time they spend outside
taking part in worship. Still less should the church attempt to
provide occupations and amusements to fill all hours outside
worship. Members are to help one another in the difficult task
of learning to live, particularly with that part of living which
remains after the hours spent in worship and daily work. There
is an old saying to the effect that any fool can work but that it
takes a wise man to enjoy and profit by leisure. Christians have
to learn how to live by experiment and error consequent upon
revelation. God so loves us that he will not suffer the error to
reign: no doubt errors often give immediate satisfaction for the
immediate moment but the immediate moment is only a
moment. Always the group of Christians at a local centre have
to arrange the place and time for public worship and what they
are to do outside those times both in respect of one another and
of their non-Christian acquaintances, friends and colleagues at
work. In doing so they are to remember that a community is
not maintained by the number of its corporate acts but by the
quality of its corporate acts. We know that when the bread is
broken and the word is spoken here are corporate activities of
incalculable value. Outside worship the church's most
distinctive corporate work is through her representatives: the
Member of Parliament, the ward sister, the playwright, the city
councillor, the teacher, the shop assistant . . . they do not
represent the church by insisting on the ultimate importance of
church-going and love of the church for its own sake. We want
men and women to believe in God and to accept the church
because of that belief; indeed, church life in some local centres
takes great belief in God to overcome the temptations it
presents by attempts to do the topical thing or to preserve a
way of church life suited to the 1930s or 1940s, or by having a
generally drab, apologetic air. The Gospel gives us two
pictures of corporate church life: the wedding reception at Cana
in Galilee and the Upper Room, but these two pictures must be
looked at with a third – the solitary figure on the Cross at the

Place of a Skull; here is the act that is both the most solitary act and the most corporate act that can be considered. Perhaps it was made less solitary by the presence of Mary and John, uncomprehending though they were. But on reflection all his acts in his earthly ministry were solitary and corporate at the same time; picture him breaking bread in the Upper Room with those who had so lately argued as to which should dominate and who so uncomprehendingly participated in the shared broken loaf with him. Picture him receiving the cheers of his followers as he came to the city gates, as he bore a sorrow which they could not share with him then. Picture him crashing over the tables in the Court of the Gentiles; who knew what he intended? His act at once joined and separated him from those who approved.

There is for us both aloneness and corporateness in our most significant acts done in his name. Through this we see, however dimly, a great deal about the nature of the corporate life of the church whose members, like the members of a human body, do not realise how the movements of one member affect the wellbeing or otherwise of the whole body. Members do not know precisely how they affect the life of all who live outside the church by default or ignorance of its existence.

EDUCATION AND RELIGION

He entered the city which expressed the height of Jewish culture in that generation. The white Temple buildings dominated the scene, its towers golden in the sun. The Temple enclosure was divided in two; a third was occupied by the Temple building itself and the remaining two thirds given over to the Court of the Gentiles. A colonnaded walk stretched practically the whole way round this open court. In the shelter of this walk the rabbis taught; it was here that Mary and Joseph found Jesus both hearing and questioning the rabbis. It was here that S. Paul came from Tarsus to be a pupil of Gamaliel. This Temple teaching was roughly the equivalent of our university. This combined with the teaching given to boys at local synagogues comprised the Jewish education system at the time of our Lord. In a theocracy, as in Jerusalem, religion and education could not be separated from one another. So it was that the nation was kept conscious of the glories of the past, as well as the times of leanness, captivity and threatened extinction. Together with remembrance of the past were the hopes for the future and longings for signs of the collapse of Rome and the nation's restoration to full independence. The simple and pious were patient but many grew tired of waiting for the day of the Lord. In a modern way of putting it: the nation's solidarity was preserved by the political astuteness of statesmen in submission to Rome on the most favourable terms and the combined policy of religious and educational leaders. But the formal education was slight and the number of educated people small. In our age we are concerned with formal education and the desirability of increasing the amount of education given to each individual.

The Jews were not disturbed about illiteracy. Lack of formal education was made up by a certain amount of informal education. Men and women learned a great deal by ploughing, sowing crops, digging, building, looking after sheep, buying and selling in small villages or in the Jerusalem shops, the equivalent of our Harrods, Fortnum and Mason and so on. Men and women learned a great deal through loving and hating one another, mourning for one another and rejoicing with one another. It is difficult in life to think of any human activity in which there is not a process of teaching and learning with the role of teacher and pupil continually interchanging. The more civilized people become the more they tend to interpret their experiences of things and other people. As it is impossible to translate literally one language into another so it is impossible to find words to describe one's experiences; indeed the more important the experience the more inadequate any attempt to describe it in words. Yet we must go on trying to make sense of our experience in order to achieve enough coherency of mind to live significantly. Education does not provide us with a set of extra experiences which run parallel to or between our other experiences; education attempts to provide the experience of understanding the totality of our experiences which widens and deepens our awareness of the vast uncharted territories of reality. Great educationalists excite a reverence for human knowledge without ever losing sight of the fact that every advance in human knowledge opens up a new field of human ignorance. Education, as opposed to mere instruction, extends both human knowledge and human ignorance as it encourages us to find in the partially known that which is less partially known.

When education is at its best it develops a state of mind which is capable of widening and deepening the devoutness of the religious and also capable of helping the irreligious to a state where religion may be recognised as a possible and real way of living. This always can happen where the awe-inspiring mystery of being is disclosed with its consequent realization of the greatness and smallness of men. For the religious man education represents a type of adoration for it entails the discovery of God who is all that is in all. For the religious man education is a study of theology because he is led to reflection on the goodness and evil in all things and in people who corrupt things. The religious man knows that he must continue his study of reality even though his faith be endangered in doing so because the Lord teaches us that whosoever tries to save himself will lose himself: he will lose himself in the amorphous company of the vague or be found among those who cannot pray and cannot leave the gate that leads to truth, or rather to him who is truth, the path by which it is reached and the power of every traveller.

We must have a theory of human vocation which lays down no narrow qualifications and which presupposes difference in natural endowment, abilities and spiritual gifts. Consequently we must avoid even the appearance of implying that only the intellectually able and well-educated can be religious, that is, capable of a full response to the vocation to be human. Both religion and education are tested by accepting or refusing to accept the fact that some of us will remain beginners. In any cross-section of society there will always be a percentage of the ineducable and a percentage of unspiritual people who have not known any such experience as the psalmist who said 'My soul is athirst for the living God'. The mature educationalist or pastor does not set out to change people but to enable them to be more fully what they are.

Too much formal education in religion dulls the ring of gospel truth. Education is at its height whenever individuals find out where education fails. Religion is at its height when individuals realize that the fundamental vocation is not to be religious but to be human. Education is at its best when people are mentally and spiritually enlivened through it, and religion is at its highest when religious people forget they are religious through their delight in living the style of life which religion reveals.

On the first Palm Sunday our Lord accepted the cheers of a very mixed crowd in a holiday mood. He always accepts the burst of praise of those who express their joy in living the life he makes possible rather than the measured prayers of those who are intent on avoiding sin and finding people who need the sort of help that can be given simply. Education and religion do work together when they combine to give us a taste for the kind of life that is more and other than morality and kindliness.

POLITICAL REALISM

He came to his own home and his
own people received him not

JOHN 1 11

'Teacher, we know that you are true,
and teach the way of God truthfully,
and care for no man; for you do not
regard the position of men. Tell
us, then, what you think. Is
it lawful to pay taxes to Caesar,
or not?'

MATTHEW 22 16-17

We can imagine our Lord surrounded by an eager crowd straining to catch every word he spoke. His followers are thrilled by his obvious success demonstrated by his challenge to the rulers in magnificent gesture when the tables were flung over and the traders and money-changers backed away in fear. All of a sudden it appeared that this might be the moment and this might be the man to banish the Romans and bring the profitable caution of the Sadducees to an end. Some might have that attitude and others vaguely expected something to happen, following him about the courtyard excited and ready for anything. He had his bodyguard in the form of a crowd of the common people. The authorities dare not lay hands on him as long as the unruly crowd remained with him. The emissaries of the rulers were seen to be moving with slow measured steps while the crowd opened up to make a pathway for them to come to him. They were urbane, the question was reasonable, patriotic. Is it lawful to pay tribute to Caesar or not? He knew the trap at once. If he said No, some of those who listened would cheer and he could be taken and held on a charge of inciting the people to rebel against their Roman masters. If he said Yes, the crowd would shrivel in size at such a disappointment. They would lose interest in someone who joined the upper classes in a safety first political policy. The dispossessed class in any society are too sullen and bitter to support a system which keeps its members in poverty; rebellion could not leave them worse off than the hated safety which kept the rich rich if not enabling them to become richer. You can imagine the hush to hear the question, the buzz of comment after it and the deeper hush that fell on the crowd waiting for his answer: 'Why put me to the test you hypocrites? Shew me the money for the tax . . . Whose likeness and inscription is this?' He held the coin up in his hand, people stretched to look and listen – a coin had become important beyond its worth, it became a symbol for the past, future and present for Hebrews and Romans. 'Whose likeness and inscription is this?' They said, 'Caesar's'. The crowd grew more intent for his reply. It was this: 'Render therefore to Caesar the things that are Caesar's, and to God the things that are God's.'

The questioners departed without a word. There was nothing to say. Did the crowd begin to depart from him too? One can only speculate and the truth cannot be balanced on speculations; it crushes them. We know that he was rejected by each class of the community in turn; just before the end his own disciples forsook him and fled and a stranger carried his cross along the Via Dolorosa. Yet he was never alone, as he said himself; his aloneness joined him to the whole of humanity in a way that could never be achieved if he had degenerated into a benign conventional person who never caused the slightest surprise by anything he said or did.

We picture our Lord standing in the middle of the crowd facing his questioners, holding the coin in his hand. As we look and think we realise that in saying 'Render to Caesar the things that are Caesar's' he was encouraging people to go on paying taxes to Romans although part of their tax money would go to support the most efficient war machine in the ancient world. Someone might say that in a complex situation the best course of action was to support the Pax Romana even though it meant maintaining the Roman armies, but that was preferable to uproar, violence and chaos. A good many of us would describe his answer as political realism both from the aspect of international and national affairs. Born at the time he was born our Lord loved his country and would share in a longing for national independence. He would see that any attempt to fight Rome could only end in debacle and desolation. Therefore the only possible course was to maintain the status quo, fragile and uncertain as it was. Submission never seems heroic whereas defiance always does. Our Lord

could have become a popular hero had he chosen to lead the
resistance force which flourished chiefly in Galilee. But heroism
is often bought at the cost of truth, that is by the invention of a
necessity as distinct from the necessity that exists. The
Crucifixion was not sought by our Lord for its own sake, but it
became inevitable once he lived his mission in the real situation
of his day. The creative power of his mission is seen in the
emergence of a small group out of the Hebrew community
which grew and spread at an amazing speed all over the
Roman empire, and has lived through the ups and downs of
two thousand years. His answer about the tribute money was
one of the vivid ways of demonstrating the truth that the
church is always to grasp the implications of being a company
of people who live here on earth as those who live in two
worlds, the worlds indicated by his words 'Render to Caesar
the things that are Caesar's and to God the things that are
God's.' In every age the Christian must ask and answer the
question 'What are Caesar's things? What are God's things?'
The answers are not merely made in words but through the
style of a life lived. In our age we are passing out of the stage of
national grouping into international groupings, akin to the
church's way of living, for our ties are not ties of blood and
place of birth but the ties of Baptism. In the meantime, we in
this country must see and give Caesar his things in a welfare
state and some of us are perturbed because Caesar seems to
have many of the things we should be rendering to God. In
getting accustomed to our present situation we have to ask
ourselves 'Is Caesar an enemy of God by his very office? Is God
the enemy of Caesar? What has Caesar that God has not given
him?' In the meantime we pay income tax, health insurance,
city rates and puzzle ourselves over the growth and
development of an affluent society. We regard the state's
provision of hospitals, schools, medical attention outside
hospitals and all the other provisions, and the growing
importance and influence of physicists, psychiatrists, artists,
entertainers and advertising agents, and wonder if our religion
is being indirectly attacked or benefitted. We wonder thus
because we are concerned with the church's mission; we
cannot forget that we are both called and sent; nor can we
forget that whoever receives us receives him that sent us. We
are not sent to take people out of the world but to send them

deeper into it, by opening their eyes and stirring their pride in their vocation to be human.

In fulfilling our mission we are to love the world as God loves it and to find him in it. But whenever we enjoy the good things of the world we must remember its ungodliness. We must also remember its goodness when we are painfully aware of its ungodliness. We have always to remember the whole muddle of goodness and evil and resist the desire to see clear black and white. To use gospel figures of speech, the wheat and the tares, the sheep and the goats, grow up, indistinguishable from one another, in prolific confusion. We must abhor a greed for clarity of mind and distinctive action and rejoice in the light and bear what it discloses to the faithful. We are taught that love is more important than knowledge and that knowledge is good when it enhances our love. Knowledge is not to be sought for its own sake; therefore we set out to know what is Caesar's and what is God's that we may love in truth, always recognising that criticism, even adverse criticism, is one of the authentic expressions of love.

SALT AND LIGHT

And he sent two of his disciples,
and said to them, "Go into the city,
and a man carrying a jar of water
will meet you: follow him, and
wherever he enters, say to the
householder, the Teacher says, 'Where
is my guest room where I am to
eat the passover with my disciples?'
And he will show you a large upper
room furnished and ready . . ."

MARK 14 13-15

The rejection of our Lord is seen and partly understood as we picture the growing hostility in the Court of the Gentiles, the arrest in the Garden, the trial and condemnation, the cross at the Place of a Skull. We see the acceptance of our Lord as we picture him seated at table as a friend with his friends. A short time before supper began these friends of his were arguing as to which of them should be greatest. They argued as to which of them should do the most important things and hold the highest office. They could not be said to have earned their friendship with him through good conduct. No one earns friendship from another. Friendship is made by the people concerned in it and it is an attraction of person for person rather than the inevitable result of two people helping one another in trouble over a certain length of time. We like people for what they are and not on account of what they do, even if what they do is for us. Our religion shows this attitude to us in countless ways but particularly in the Upper Room as we picture the disciples moving slowly and awkwardly to take their places at table after their argument. These men had left their business, their home, their place in society to be with him and humanlike they felt that there must be some return, and when Peter put a question to their Master about this expectation he was given a dark answer in terms of the reward being misery, hardship and added responsibility for a great many people. This contented them for the time; it had to because he rarely did more than answer a simple-looking question in a most complicated way, specially when he was leading them into some understanding

of a way of life in which a man lost what he kept and kept what
he gave; a life in which there was neither buying nor selling,
where people discovered that the only things worth having
were the things no one could deserve. Probably they blushed
when something of the wonder of this way of life possessed
them as they took their place at table hoping he had missed the
gist of their argument.

Here at table were the men who were called by our Lord and
who responded to his call. No one is only interested in their
characteristic temptations and factual reports of their sins. We
are more concerned with what they were intended to be. John
the Baptist was described as the voice of one crying in the
wilderness. In the Sermon on the Mount in Matthew 5 the
disciples were told to be the light of the world and the salt of the
earth and to remember that they were a city on a hill that could
not be hidden. They were told to be the light of their world.
They had not to make the light they bore into the darkness;
they were not told to try to attract attention to themselves; they
were to be light and others would be both illuminated and
warmed. This is the poetic way of describing the life of a
disciple, making it clear that the good life is something other
than living with an attitude towards sin, an alertness to notice
those in need of help and a readiness to be a good influence on
all men. This is not denying that a disciple must be aware of his
sinfulness or that he should be willing to help his neighbour
and interested in the influence he bears on others. 'You are the
light of the world'. That is, do not be over-much concerned
with the results of your work being the light, rather 'Let your
light so shine before men that they may see your good works
and glorify your Father which is in heaven'. The religious life is
more than concern for sin, people who need help and being a
good influence. It is an expression of power, love, compassion,
glory combining into a single splendour through the grace of
God. Let the light shine, make no calculations about its
brightness or the effect it should have or seems to have. There
is a spontaneity in all authentic Christian living; there can,
obviously, be no direct way of acquiring spontaneity; one may
be given it through forgetting it in love of life and men and
God and self in the way that faith makes possible and with the
stability that hope makes firm. A disciple spreads a love of life
even in the hour of death. The supper table on Maundy

Thursday night shows the unconquerable One giving the bread
of life to men growing out of their timidity . . . He said of himself,
'I am the light of the world'. He said to the disciples, 'You are the
light of the world; you are not to hide your light, let it shine'. In
other words, do not apologetically offer your knowledge of life
and death; it is to be shared not justified. A Christian never
commends the Gospel by drawing attention to himself. The
message makes the man, not the man the message.

'You are the salt of the earth.'

Salt preserves what is good, heals wounds and flavours food.
Salt preserves, heals, flavours. Our Lord said that he came to
fulfil, not to destroy, the law and the prophets. His disciples are
not to destroy the best things in the culture of their generation;
we are to appreciate the work of scientists, artists, legislators
and social workers without giving our unqualified approval
because all the works of men are marred by human finiteness
and human sin. In our greatest actions our clumsiness and
sinfulness are both exposed and not all of the clumsiness and
sinfulness is the agent's: we never act in isolation, privately or
in the presence of spectators; others always participate or
hinder. Salt preserves the good. Disciples are to preserve the
significant importance of human acts not by talking out their
importance but by acting. Salt heals. Disciples are to have
power to heal. Only the broken can heal; only those whose false
self-sufficiency is broken can be sufficient enough to heal. The
power to comfort belongs to those who bear sorrow. Salt
flavours. Insipid food is unpalatable, so is a man's life when it is
bound up in routine. Only those who do not despise small
essential tasks can deliver others out of routine become prison.
Disciples have a mission to those who bore others and to those
who are bored. Boredom is the result of living over and over the
same small mental routine movements. The tang of salt, the
biting flavour brings freshness to all who are tired of life, as
well as to all who are not fully alive yet. The Christian is to live
creatively in that he spreads a love of life wherever he goes, not
because he has avoided the knowledge that is capable of
saddening or defiling but because he knows men and still loves
them. St. John says that if a man cannot love his brother whom
he has seen how can he love God whom he has not seen. It is

just because we have seen and known our brother that we find
it difficult to love him. It does not do if Christians content
themselves with telling themselves that they love abstractions
like 'everybody', 'all classes, creeds and races'. They are to love
those particular people they are nearest to in association, being
ready to add particular persons as our destiny demands. We are
to go on loving people in their vagueness, their muddle or
rightness and wrongness, their self-seeking, their readiness to
be parasites or to patronize, their splendour, their shame,
timidity and foolhardiness. All are made in the image of God,
no matter how distorted or defaced the image may be. Our love
for them is not flavoured with saccharine or sugar but with salt,
and persists no matter what response they make.

Our Lord used the figure of speech at a time and in a country
where salt was costly. So disciples are to preserve, heal, flavour
and also to remember their worth. It is not Christian humility to
draw attention to your smallness and inadequacy but to be
great according to the gift that is within you. Our Lord said to
the disciples, 'You are the light of the world. A city set on a hill
cannot be hid'.

All our Lord ever said to his disciples during his earthly
ministry went to make their mission in the world clear. Their
thoughts about themselves and their prayers were to feed and
be sustained by their words and deeds. Their doctrine was to
illuminate their deeds and their deeds were to make their
doctrine lucid. That is, their thoughts, prayers, words and
deeds were all to be parts of a single unity of living the life he
described in terms of a man loving God, his neighbour and
himself. In the Sermon on the Mount this unity of living was
described as salt and light. What they were to do was to be
carefree, specially as God would bring all real work to the best
of all conclusions. Wherever the light shines it does all that
light should do; similarly when salt is used it acts as salt should.
Our Lord leaves us with no illusions about the nature of our
responsibility – 'A city set on a hill cannot be hid'; 'If salt has lost
its taste, how shall its saltness be restored?'

'A city set on a hill cannot be hid'. The church must have a
visible form. It needs buildings, it needs fixed places for its
worship, it needs a form of worship out of which the formal life
of the fellowship crystallizes. We regret dilapidated buildings,
ugly stained glass and sentimental music. We regret the

clumsiness and heretical distortion of forms of worship. We deplore whenever the fellowship is no more than a gathering of people round the altar feeling no connection between what they do there with what they think and talk about and do once they cross the threshold of the church into the city street. We regret when the word spoken in the pulpit is little other than a decent humanism with implications about the Christian conception of worship and behaviour left unclear. But this is not the norm. There are churches which express the intangible things which are to be found at that point where the temporal and eternal are experienced as one. Outsiders and enquirers see the church as clearly as a city on a hill top. We cannot be hidden for good or for ill. Our holiness, our splendour, our folly, our love, our pride, our nobility, our decay and impenitence, our humility and love of truth and justice are all seen in a muddle as people look for the quality of the church in each of us who represent (literally represent) the church wherever we go in whatever company we are. In our eagerness to be the best representative possible we must not be found self-conscious about our task and we must not be found telling lies in order that man may respect the church as an institution which preserves the truth of the Gospel. Such lying is very seldom deliberate and deals chiefly with the alleged goodness of church members and the efficacy of the church's power to heal the mentally distraught. But holiness does not mean sinlessness; it is as characteristic of church members to be penitent as to give firm statements of the faith that is within them. The church is a tree that bears both corrupt and incorrupt fruit but the corrupt is more than balanced by the good fruit. Here fruit is taken as the thoughts, words and deeds of its members either corporately or individually. This needs to be considered frequently as so many, inside and outside ecclesiastical circles, will equate being religious with being morally irreproachable, just as so many will consider that Christianity soothes but does not disturb and are quick to see the church as a therapeutic agent to follow up the cures begun by psychiatrists. It would be a poor day if the church had no gift or concern for the broken, the outcast and the criminal; the church has, if she is also ready to meet the strong, the brilliant, the charming and the successful in life on their own ground. Of course in different ages and in different places the church is frail in its expression of the life that sets men free. We have been warned: if the salt have lost its savour wherewith shall it be salted? It is thenceforth good for nothing, but to be cast out and trodden under the foot of men.

Let us look again at the men seated at the supper table with our Lord. The light of the world? The city set on a hill? The salt of the earth? They wondered which of them should do the most important thing; one of them left and closed the door behind him; one denied that he even knew his Master; they all ran and left him in the awful moment when their safety counted more to them than anything else. But they returned; having once known life with him no other kind of life was possible for them.

EPILOGUE

The Shadow of the Cross[1]

"By the wood of the Cross the work of the Word of God was
made manifest to all: his hands are stretched out to gather all
men together"   St. Irenaeus

Beneath the shadow of the Cross
My genius stands reproved.
All the clever things I could say about him turn to ashes in my
mouth,
All the ways I could justify myself are called in question by that
silent figure.
If only he would cry out and condemn me!
But there is nothing, only this silence and this darkness.
Beneath the shadow of the Cross
My genius stands reproved.

How often would I decry the Passion as a folly or a fairy-tale.
Beneath the shadow of the Cross
My wisdom stands reproved.
How often, like Pilate, would I wash my hands of the whole
business and enjoy myself and forget.

Beneath the shadow of the Cross
My triviality stands reproved.
How often, like Judas, would I prefer the darkness of night to
the fellowship of Light.
Beneath the shadow of the Cross
My self-will stands reproved.
How often, like Thomas, would I demand full knowledge of all
mysteries.
Beneath the shadow of the Cross
My haughtiness stands reproved.
How often, like John, would I be close to him through the
demands of every occasion.
Beneath the shadow of the Cross
My love stands fortified.

On every thought, on every wish, on every word, on every
deed, on every prayer
    There falls the shadow of the Cross.

    I do not stand alone within it, I cannot –
    I stand a member of the human family and of the Church of
    God.
    Beneath the shadow of the Cross
    Our disunity stands reproved.

Christ the crucified is Christ the King, Christ the Judge.
    We cannot deny his power,
    We dare not deny his mercy.
    Beneath the shadow of the Cross
    Complacency is shattered.

How often would we turn away to chide God for his seeming
inactivity
And clamour for his work to be done at our speed.
    Beneath the shadow of the Cross
    Our hurry and impatience stand reproved.

Take my yoke upon you . . . Take my burden, says the Lord, the
Crucified.
He who would be my disciple, let him take up his cross;
In his obedience he shall be shown the occasions of his slow
crucifixion –
The scorn, the shady treachery, the silent contempt, the
heedless passer by . . .

    Nothing in my hand I bring
    Simply to thy Cross I cling:
    That nothing must be something,
    Something which costs me a lot
    And I must not forget the cost.

    Beneath the shadow of the Cross
    My genius stands reproved.

[1]A meditation used at a Student Christian Movement in
Schools conference in 1953.

1	2	3	4	5	6	7	8	9	10	11	12	13	14	15	16	17	18	19	20
21	22	23	24	25	26	27	28	29	30	31	32	33	34	35	36	37	38	39	40
41	42	43	44	45	46	47	48	49	50	51	52	53	54	55	56	57	58	59	60
61	62	63	64	65	66	67	68	69	70	71	72	73	74	75	76	77	78	79	80
81	82	83	84	85	86	87	88	89	90	91	92	93	94	95	96	97	98	99	100
101	102	103	104	105	106	107	108	109	110	111	112	113	114	115	116	117	118	119	120
121	122	123	124	125	126	127	128	129	130	131	132	133	134	135	136	137	138	139	140
141	142	143	144	145	146	147	148	149	150	151	152	153	154	155	156	157	158	159	160
161	162	163	164	165	166	167	168	169	170	171	172	173	174	175	176	177	178	179	180
181	182	183	184	185	186	187	188	189	190	191	192	193	194	195	196	197	198	199	200